THE CHANGING
RAILWAYS
OF BRITAIN

PAUL HURLEY AND PHIL BRAITHWAITE

THE CHANGING
RAILWAYS
OF BRITAIN

FROM STEAM TO DIESEL AND ELECTRIC

The
History
Press

First published 2019

The History Press
The Mill, Brimscombe Port
Stroud, Gloucestershire, GL5 2QG
www.thehistorypress.co.uk

British Library Cataloguing in Publication Data.
A catalogue record for this book is available from the British Library.

ISBN 978 0 7509 8982 4

Typesetting and origination by The History Press
Printed and bound in India by Thomson Press India Ltd

Above: Two Class 31 diesel locomotives entering Bristol Temple Meads station in 1978. The numbers are unknown, but the two hard-working old diesels are hauling a passenger train as opposed to the goods duties they are used to.

Half title page: It is getting near to the end of steam on BR and 66019 *Bittern* is seen here at Stockport Edgeley shed in 1966. It is being prepared for the William Deacons bank excursion; steam traction was in demand for rail tours long before steam ended.

Frontispiece: A little more up to date now with the first of the new-build engines 60163 *Tornado*, seen at York station on 3 July 2013. It was built mainly at Darlington Works; the work started in 1994 and was completed in 2008. It is the only existing example of an LNER Peppercorn-designed A1 locomotive, as all the original production batch was scrapped!

Overleaf: The locomotive peeping from Patricroft shed in 1966 is a Riddles-designed Standard Class 4 4-6-0 No. 75029, built at Swindon in 1954. This was only one of five Class 4 MT locomotives to be built with a double chimney. When it was withdrawn in August 1967, it was purchased by the artist David Shepherd, who sold it to the North Yorkshire Moors Railway in 1998, where it was renamed *The Green Knight*.

Jacket illustrations: *Front, top:* Black Five 4-6-0 No. 45303 at Warrington Bank Quay station; *Front, bottom:* Class 40 1Co-Co1 D277 at Derby, hauled by a steam engine. *Back:* Bo-Bo Class 81 No. E3014 passing through Crewe.

FROM A RAILWAY CARRIAGE

Faster than fairies, faster than witches
Bridges and houses, hedges and ditches,
All through the meadows the horses and cattle;
All of the sights of the hill and the plain
Fly as thick as driving rain;
And ever again in the wink of an eye,
Painted stations whistle by.
Here is a child who clambers and scrambles,
All by himself and gathering brambles;
Here is a tramp who stands and gazes,
And there is the green for stringing the daisies;
Here is a cart run away in the road
Lumping along with man and load;
And here is a mill and there is a river;
Each a glimpse and gone forever!

Robert Louis Stevenson
A Child's Garden of Verses

CONTENTS

Acknowledgements   8

About the Authors   8

Introduction   9

1   Steam: The Workhorse of the Industrial Revolution   11

2   Electricity Arrives on the Scene   25

3   Time for a Look at Diesel Traction   29

4   A Nationalised British Railways Comes into Existence   49

5   A Mix of Motive Power   56

6   A Decision is Made: Stick with Steam for the Time Being   66

7   Have to Change Tack and Dump Steam   80

8   A Look at Diesel and Electric Multiple Units   87

9   Still with Diesel Traction but a Bit More Colourful   97

10 More Up-to-Date Motive Power   107

11 Modern Passenger Stock   111

12 Preserved Lines and Stock   119

    Epilogue   144

ACKNOWLEDGEMENTS

With the photographs taken by Phil, there are not many people to mention. I must mention, however, the administrators of two websites which are both excellent sources of information and who allowed me to dip into them as part of my research: Ian Jenkins of the BRDataBase and Howie Milburn from the RailUK database. I must also thank Anthony Coulls, the senior curator of the York and Locomotion museums. Thanks as well to our commissioning editor Amy Rigg and our project editor Jezz Palmer for their support and advice, and finally our wives, Rose and Helen, for their patience.

ABOUT THE AUTHORS

Paul Hurley is a writer and member of the Society of Authors. He has contributed to *Railway* and other magazines and has written an award-winning novel, as well as twenty-four local history books. He is married to Rose and has two sons and two daughters. He lives in Winsford, Cheshire.

Phil Braithwaite has been a railway photographer since the late 1950s, both in the UK and South Africa, photographing the last of steam traction. He is the owner of a Thomas Green & Son 1924 steamroller and van. Phil lives with his wife Helen in Barnton, Cheshire.

Their previous book for The History Press was *Remembering Steam: The End of British Rail Steam in Photographs*.

INTRODUCTION

Before the end of steam, the odd engine was preserved by the British Transport Commission and later the British Railways Board and passed into the custody of the Curator of Historical Relics. These were locomotives intended to be nothing more than static displays in the Clapham Railway Museum and at Butlins holiday camps! Those running the railways grossly underestimated the interest there was then and that there would be in the coming years after the days of steam had come to an end in August 1968.

What British film of the period, if not featuring a steam train, didn't have the many sounds of one in the background? The sound of a goods train working hard in the distance on a still summer night … A night express thundering past, the glow from the firebox reflecting from the passing lineside … And for enthusiasts, the sheer enjoyment of standing at the end of the platform watching the numerous classes, shapes and sounds of steam engines passing through, many with brass nameplates, nameplates that could be purchased relatively cheaply at the time. Original ones will now sell for what a locomotive sold for in the 1950s and '60s. Musty carriages, slam doors and curly butties in the buffet all add to a bank of memories that people thought would be all that would be left after 1968. BR wanted to look forward to the future of a clean and modern rail system. Just one steam engine had bucked the rules when Alan Pegler had managed to make an arrangement in which he could use *Flying Scotsman* on the main line until 1972.

Thanks to the foresight of many hard-working volunteers, enthusiasts managed to acquire enough financial support to purchase a locomotive from British Rail, who (it has to be said) did not make it easy for them. Even harder was the acquisition of lengths of closed line and even a station or two, but they kept at it as steam locomotives were being scrapped at a fast rate. Engines with a life expectancy of forty years were being cut up after serving for fewer than ten. But these early preservationists were a hardy bunch, and fortunately much was saved thanks also to Dai Woodham and his

scrapyard in Barry, South Wales. He scrapped a few locomotives but stored the rest, concentrating upon scrapping wagons. Over the next twenty or so years, his rapidly deteriorating stock was targeted by the preservation societies and private individuals. Thanks to this, he was responsible for enabling more than 200 locomotives to be saved. As the number of preserved lines grew, so an organisation called the Association of Railway Preservation Societies came into being under the initial leadership of Captain Peter Manisty RN. A diesel locomotive was named after him, and there is an annual award to preservation societies called the Peter Manisty award.

The years passed, more and more engines were rescued, mainly from Woodhams, and in the 1970s the locomotives that had spent their time as static exhibits, or features at Butlins holiday camps and other locations, came into the preservation fold. It was onwards and upwards, and the interest in steam was passed on from father to sons and daughters. Something the British Railways Board (BRB) had neither wanted or anticipated came into being: steam continued to be interesting! So interesting, in fact, that new steam engines have and still are being built. It has to be admitted that diesel and electric are cleaner and easier to maintain and drive, although whether money was saved by switching from steam is doubtful. For one thing, it was cheaper to build steam engines.

BRB continued to lose money and still needed government support, but with roads becoming more and more crowded these days the many closed lines could now be revenue earning. With diesel and electric perhaps, but revenue earning nonetheless. At the time of writing our railway network is mainly privatised, although how long that will last is questionable.

But first back to the beginning. Rudimentary experiments in the use of steam power went as far back as the Romans, but not until 1712 and Thomas Newcomen's atmospheric engine did anyone get close to commercial success. His engine was used to pump water out of coal mines. Later, steam replaced other forms of power for static use in mills, mines and the like but, although experiments had been carried out, there had been no success with making a wheeled vehicle using steam power. In the 1700s tramways pulled by horses ran firstly on wooden rails and then cast iron and steel. Railway travel in those days was not the most comfortable. Initially, passengers travelled in open wagons without even the luxury of seating.

Things changed very slowly, at least for the working classes. The upper classes, however, had flat wagons upon which their horse-drawn coach could be placed. Later still, first class carriages appeared, still in the shape of horse-drawn carriages. The make-up of passenger trains continued to improve slowly with first, second and third classes that each in its turn became more comfortable and protected from the weather. Britain tended to use individual compartments well into the 1960s that were not perhaps the best layout. Other countries such as the USA preferred open carriages as we see today, and this avoided the many complaints that arose from the abuse of people trapped in single compartments. The shape and power of locomotives continued to change as 'railway mania' took effect, although locomotives built in the late 1800s were still in revenue-earning use up until the end of steam. In this book, we shall travel through the years to the end of steam and beyond, initially through photographs of replicas of the locomotives in use at the time from Richard Trevithick and his early effort to mainline Virgin Pendolinos and other traction used on the privatised lines.

Talking of privatised lines, in the early days of the railways they were all privatised and remained so through thick and thin until British Railways was nationalised in 1948. There had been partial nationalisation during the two wars when the government took over supervision of the railways. Between the wars, in 1923 the diverse companies were amalgamated into the Big Four, then in 1948, we had full nationalisation. It was then British Railways until 1994, when privatisation returned, and by 1997 it had been completed. Gone was the standard appearance of both locomotives and carriages and in came the vibrant mix of schemes that could be seen throughout the country. In all, thirteen separate companies took over the rail franchise across the country. Railtrack purchased all the privatised rail, control of the larger stations and infrastructure and then went bust in 2001. Its duties were taken over by state-owned Network Rail – nationalisation is creeping in!

Our last book, *Remembering Steam*, took us up to the end of regular steam working. *The Changing Railways of Britain* takes us beyond that to the present day, but never forgets to look back at what came before.

Steam engines were given names like *Puffing Billy*, which was built in 1813 for the owner of Wylam Colliery in Northumberland. *Puffing Billy* was the earliest locomotive to run by adhesion to the track as opposed to rack and pinion, and the earliest in the world to do so commercially. It hauled coal from the colliery to the docks at Lemington, Newcastle upon Tyne, and remained in service until 1862. It is the oldest engine still in existence and is kept at the Science Museum, London; its sister engine, *Wylam Dilly*, is also preserved, and can be found at the National Museum of Scotland. A working replica of *Puffing Billy* is used at Beamish, and another is at the Royal Bavarian State Railway workshops. This leads us to one of the most respected railway engineers, George Stephenson, who acquired the title 'Father of the Railways' in 1814. He designed the locomotive *Blucher* and then the *Locomotion No. 1*, the latter for the Stockton and Darlington railway, which became the first passenger-carrying public steam railway in the world. But there was an earlier attempt.

◄ A replica of Richard Trevithick's first railway engine, for Coalbrookdale in 1803

The first true wheeled railway locomotive was built by Richard Trevithick in 1804. Trevithick had studied the work of William Murdoch and Nicolas-Joseph Cugnot, who had both built working models of a steam-driven road locomotive in the late 1700s. Trevithick's locomotive then became the first in the world to haul a train along the short track at the Penydarren Ironworks in Merthyr Tydfil, South Wales. Over the next few years, attempts were made to build an engine suitable for hauling trains; none were particularly successful, although *Salamanca*, a rack engine built by Mathew Murray for the Middleton Railway in Leeds, came close as it was able to haul a coal train. It was later destroyed when its boiler blew up! Left is a working replica of Richard Trevithick's engine, seen here at the Black Country Museum, in 2007.

▲ A replica of Robert Stephenson's *Rocket* originally built in 1829

Robert Stephenson, George's son, had built *Rocket* in time for the Rainhill Trials in 1829, and it had won the prize. This was given the fact that it both came first and was the only one to finish. The following year, when the Liverpool and Manchester Railway opened the inaugural run was blighted when *Rocket* ran over the MP For Liverpool William Husskison, who became the first death caused by a railway engine when he died of his injuries soon after. Robert Stephenson had returned from university to join his father in building the line. In 1829, Robert became the chief engineer of the London and Birmingham Railway and went on to become a bridge and railway builder at home and abroad, gaining the reputation as the greatest engineer of the nineteenth century. The 'feeding frenzy', or 'railway mania' as it is usually called, started and saw people investing in and building railway lines all over the country.

Locomotives were being built at a fast pace, although at first in the same mould as the successful *Rocket*. In 1838, another locomotive called *Lion* was built in the same shape for the Liverpool and Manchester Railway, mainly for goods.

▼ *Planet replica* as seen at the Museum of Science and Industry

The *Planet* was built by Robert Stephenson and Company for the Liverpool and Manchester Railway in 1830 to a similar design as the *Rocket* but with inside cylinders. It was the precursor of a 2-2-0 type, a class that became known as the Planets. This replica was built by the Friends of the Museum of Science and Industry in 1992, and when not out on the rails it can be seen within the museum.

▲ *Lion*, seen here at the Rocket 150 Cavalcade in May 1980, under its own steam

The technology was progressing if the overall design was not, as *Lion* could travel at 45mph. It was built by Todd, Kitson and Laird, which later became the engineering company Kitson, and is seen here at the National Railway Museum in York in 2016.

Lion worked on the Liverpool and Manchester Railway, which was later incorporated into the Grand Junction Railway, from 1838 to 1859, at which time it was sold to the Mersey Docks and Harbour Board as a stationary engine. It remained there until 1928, when it was rescued and refurbished, going into Lime Street station in Liverpool as a static exhibit. Before the Second World War, it was taken to Crewe Works, and after the war it spent time in the Liverpool and Manchester museums with time out in 1952 to star in the film *The Titfield Thunderbolt*.

Again, not a mainline engine but a full-sized 0-4-0 saddle tank, built in 1874 by Black Hawthorn and Company for a smelting plant. It was used to push wagons filled with bauxite ore into an aluminium smelting plant. Bauxite is a sedimentary rock with a high aluminium content. It is now at the National Railway Museum and attached to a Victorian coach formed to resemble three horse-drawn coaches, a style that was popular at the birth of the railways. Both engine and coach are in unrestored condition; *Bauxite No. 2* has large front buffers to accommodate trucks of various sizes.

▲ No. 3020 *Cornwall* seen here at The Severn Valley Railway, circa the mid 1990s

It was thought that the bigger the driving wheels, the faster the engine would travel with less strain. So our next engine, *Cornwall*, was built with 8ft driving wheels for express passenger work and was soon copied. It was designed by Francis Trevithick, son of Richard. Francis was by now one of the engineers of the London and North Western Railway (LNWR). He did not, arguably, enjoy the skills or reputation of his father. The *Cornwall* was built in 1847 with a 4-2-2-wheel arrangement.

In 1858 it was extensively rebuilt with a 2-2-2-wheel arrangement and was a successful express passenger engine that was still on the main lines in 1925. It became one of the first to be preserved and is now in the National Collection.

▼ Narrow gauge engine *Prince* on the Ffestiniog Railway

Engine shapes were changing as the century progressed. Gone was the *Rocket* style and the 8ft driving wheels and in came more recognisable locomotives. This is not a mainline engine but an example of the saddle tank style that became popular for small engines. *Prince* was an 0-4-0-TT (tank locomotive with tender), one of six locomotives built by George England and Company for the Ffestiniog Railway in 1863. This was one of the first successful narrow-gauge locomotives and is still at work on the line to this day. It has frequently been rebuilt, as would be expected of an engine that is around 156 years old. It was last restored in 2015 in readiness for its 150th birthday celebrations, seen here at Dinas that year.

▲ **London & North Western Railway 2-4-0 No. 790** *Hardwicke*

The final look at a big wheeler, although not with 8ft driving wheels, just 6ft 9in. Things were changing and engines were starting to look more up to date in the form of this steam locomotive and tender, designed by F.W. Webb and built at Crewe Works in 1898. It was one of 158 locomotives in the Precedent Class and was badly damaged in an accident in 1898, finally being withdrawn in 1932. It is now in the National Collection and at the time of writing on static exhibit in the York museum.

▼ **LMS 0-6-0 tank loco No. 1708**

Late nineteenth-century locomotives started to look familiar to those seen during nationalisation, especially this tank engine, which was designed by Samuel Johnson and built at Derby in 1880, going into service in June that year. On nationalisation it became No. 41708 and in 1966, after eighty-six years, it was withdrawn and fortunately saved for preservation. Like the more modern Standard 2MT 41241 behind it, withdrawn in the same year, it can be seen here at the Keighley and Worth Valley Railway in 1968.

▲ Johnson 0-6-0 No. 43295

Another Samuel Johnson offering that was built by Neilson and Company as the new century drew near. On 30 November 1891 this engine entered service, but it was not as lucky as the preceding one; it lasted until October 1961, when it was withdrawn and scrapped at Derby Works four months later. It is seen here awaiting return after doing a banking duty from the low-level sidings at the Twelve Arches south of Warrington in 1960.

▼ Class ES1, one of two electric locomotives

This electric engine described as steeplecab design was built in 1902 for the North Eastern Railway. It first ran in 1905, was withdrawn for preservation in 1964 and in 1977 was taken into the National Collection. The second of this two-locomotive class, ES2, was scrapped in 1966. ES1 can now be seen at the Shildon museum.

▲ **Ex Lambton colliery 0-6-2 tank No. 29**

At Pickering station on the North York Moors Railway in 2014 is a bespoke Kitson-designed locomotive that was built by Hunslet for the colliery in 1904. It was introduced at Philadelphia on Tyneside and withdrawn from there in 1969. It saw service at Lambton, Hetton and Joicey collieries and the National Coal Board. It is probably the oldest steam locomotive still in use and is currently at Grosmont awaiting completion of a service. There is a colour photo of the engine later in the book.

This 4-6-0, seen at Dawsholm in Glasgow in early 1964, was designed as a goods engine for the Highland Railway, whose superintendent was David Jones, hence the class name. It was built by Sharp Stewart and Company at its Atlas Works in Glasgow in 1894. They were the first British 4-6-0 locomotives and were known as Highland Railway Big Goods. In 1965, HR 103 starred in the film *Those Magnificent Men in Their Flying Machines*. It can now be found in the Scottish Museum of Transport.

▲ **Class 1500 0-6-0 Tank No. 1501**

Seen on the Mid-Norfolk Railway in 2016 is this 0-6-0 pannier tank locomotive 1501. It is the only survivor from a class of ten. Hawksworth designed the class, and they were built at Swindon Works for British Railways in 1949. No. 1501 was the first to be withdrawn in January 1961 from Southall. It was then sold with 1502 and 1509 to the National Coal Board for use at Coventry Colliery. In 1970 all three were purchased by the Severn Valley Railway, where 1502 and 1509 were used as spare parts to overhaul 1501 and then taken to Cashmores of Great Bridge for scrapping. No. 1501 is now in revenue-earning service after a further overhaul.

Diesel and electricity predominate on the metals now, but this is not new; batteries drove the very first electric locomotive that was designed by Robert Davidson of Aberdeen in 1837. He later built a larger locomotive called *Galvani* that weighed 7½ tons. It had two direct drive reluctance motors, with fixed electromagnets attached to iron bars fixed to the side. It hauled a load of 6 tons for 1½ miles (2km). The very first railway powered by electricity was Volk's Electric Railway in Brighton. It was a narrow-gauge pleasure railway that opened in 1883, having been built by Magnus Volk, and is still operational.

◀ **London Underground Train**

The next electric railway – and another record-breaker – was the London Underground, the very first underground railway in the world. However, this was not the first electrically powered railway, as it was initially run on steam. The first line built was the Metropolitan Railway, opened in 1863, and then, like the surface railways, a building frenzy started that spread the lines under London and the surrounding area. The first of these lines to be powered by electricity was the City, while South London Railway opened in 1890 and was the first deep-level underground tube railway in the world and the first full-sized railway to use electric traction. The original plan was for cables to haul the trains but, during the building of the line, the company providing the cable apparatus went bankrupt. Electricity was in its infancy at the time, especially electric traction for electric locomotives, but it was chosen and was a success.

By 1905 most tube lines had been electrified, although the Metropolitan Railway was still using steam engines to pull passenger stock. Over the following years, steam was used as departmental stock on the underground, and the last was not withdrawn until 6 June 1971. This was celebrated by a commemorative run hauled by 0-6-0 pannier tank No. L94, comprising a train of engineering vehicles from Moorgate and Barbican to Neasden depot, and Barbican was open to the public. Even now there are some preserved locomotives that are occasionally seen hauling specials.

Rather than close the line from Ryde Pier to Shanklin on the Isle of White in 1967, it was electrified, and forty-three London underground cars of standard stock were purchased. Their low height allowed for passage beneath the tunnels. In 1989 these trains were replaced by refurbished 1938 Underground stock comprising two-car Class 483 units.

▲ **Liverpool Overhead Railway carriage at the Museum of Liverpool**

Now we look at the very first overhead electric railway in the world. The Liverpool Overhead, or as described in a good old-fashioned Scouse accent, the 'dockers umbrella'. It was opened in 1893 with a raised line that ran along the Liverpool waterfront, and it was a precursor of much that we have today. It was the first elevated electric railway in the world, the first to use automatic signalling and electric light signalling, and featured one of the first passenger escalators at any railway station. This unique railway used electric multiple units – another first. One of the motor cars (driving unit and carriage) is seen at the Museum of Liverpool.

The line at first ran from Alexandra Dock to Herculaneum Dock but was later extended to Seaforth and Litherland at one end in 1894 and Dingle at the other in 1896. The Dingle station was at the end of a tunnel cut into the rockface. The opening to this tunnel can still be seen high up at the Dingle end of the Dock Road.

▼ **Route sign inside the preserved carriage and (inset) an advert for the line**

Bombing damaged the Overhead during the Second World War, and a new batch of railcars appeared in the early 1950s. By the mid '50s, the fabric of the line had deteriorated, accelerated by the Mersey Docks and Harbour steam engines that ran beneath it. At midnight on Sunday, 30 December 1956 services ceased and over the coming months it was demolished completely. An appeal is under way to rebuild it as a monorail. Another company using electric traction in the same area was the Liverpool to Southport mainline. Electric traction was becoming popular in other countries and Dick Kerr & Co. in Preston was also experimenting with electricity. In 1902 the Lancashire and Yorkshire Railway (LYR) decided to electrify the line in competition with the Cheshire Lines Committee (CLC). The LYR built the rolling stock and Dick Kerr the traction systems. The power came from a unique live third rail. The line between Liverpool and Southport began running using electricity on 22 March 1904.

▲ EM1/Class 76 electric locomotive No. 76047

The Manchester–Sheffield–Wath Railway, better known as the Woodhead Railway, was opened in 1841, having been built with Joseph Locke as its engineer. It went from Manchester to Penistone and Sheffield, and had various name changes and mergers over the years. In 1845 the first of the Woodhead tunnels were completed, the second was opened in 1853, and 100 years later in 1953, the third was finished. It was eventually quadrupled in places due to the heavy traffic. In fact, the original two Woodhead tunnels saw 250 steam trains pass through each day.

By the 1930s the heavy steam-powered coal trains were struggling to get over the Penistone Wath section, known as the Worsborough Branch, with its steep gradients and narrow tunnels. It was decided to electrify the line using 1,500 volts DC; however, the extremely narrow bores of the Woodhead Tunnels one and two meant that there was no room for the electric wires. In 1936 the plans were coming to fruition, with many of the overhead gantries completed. Then the Second World War started, and everything stopped. After the war a new double-track third Woodhead tunnel was planned to leave room for the overhead wires, and in 1953 it was opened and the other two closed to be used by the National Grid to carry their power lines.

The electrification project was completed in 1955 using 1,500 volts DC; this was superseded on other lines around the world, leaving the Woodhead line as the only one with 1.5kV electrification. The contract for the building of electric locomotives for the line was given to Gorton Works, with Manchester EM1/Class 76, as seen above, for freight trains and EM2/Class 77 for express passenger trains. Class 506 multiple units were built for the suburban services around Glossop and Hadfield. BR even built a new depot for the new electric stock at Reddish in 1954.

Despite such a major investment in electrification, new rolling stock and even a tunnel, BR decided to close the line to passenger traffic, and this it did on 5 January 1970. The Class 77 locomotives were sold to the Netherlands, and the Class 76 locomotives continued to work the line. By the 1980s it was decided that a required upgrade to the system was not worth it and the line closed completely. The tracks were lifted in the mid-1980s. The National Grid still own the three Woodhead tunnels, and a length of the trackbed is now the Longdale Trail for walkers.

No. 76047 was seen at Dinting on the Woodhead Line in the 1960s. It was built at BR Gorton and introduced in July 1951. It was withdrawn in March 1970 and cut up at Reddish by J. Cashmore in October 1971.

TIME FOR A LOOK AT DIESEL TRACTION

At the end of the Second World War, across Europe the railways were in a mess. The London, Midland and Scottish Railway (LMS) in Britain authorised the building of a pair of 1,600hp diesel locomotives and both were built at Derby Works with a Co-Co wheel configuration, the first in 1946 and the second in 1947. The engineer in charge was H.G. Ivatt. The motive power was provided by English Electric 16SVT, and the transmission was diesel-electric. The traction motors came from Dick Kerr at Preston. Both locomotives, numbered 10000 and 10001, were identical and resembled the later Deltics. They could reach 95mph and initially worked on the LMS main lines both singly and in tandem hauling passenger express trains. At nationalisation in 1949, they became

part of British Rail and were given the Class Number D16/1. They remained on the former LMS lines until 1953, when they were transferred to the Southern Region of BR to test against the second build of diesel in service Class D16/2, as featured next. In this view of the scrap line at Derby Works in 1966 we can see all of these first-built diesel locomotives. No. 10000 was withdrawn in 1963 and used as a donor for 10001. It remained at the works until it was scrapped at Cashmores of Great Bridge in January 1968, while 10001 was withdrawn in 1966 and scrapped at Cox and Danks of Acton, also in January 1968, despite many attempts to preserve at least one. In fact, 10000 was offered to the Clapham Railway Museum but it declined the offer due to a lack of space.

◀ Derby Works in 1966, 10000 and 10001 together with 10201/2 and 3

In the meantime, railway engineer Oliver Bulleid was busy planning his own prototype diesel-electric passenger engines to be built in the old Southern area. Two, 10201 and 10202 were built at Ashford Works in 1950 and 1951 and the third at Brighton Works in 1953. All three had the wheel arrangement 1Co-Co1 and were given the BR Code D16/2. All three were withdrawn at the end of 1963 and scrapped at Cashmores of Great Bridge in 1968.

▲ No. 10203 on the Derby scrap line in 1966

Both of these small prototype classes of diesel locomotives proved a great success in service and were put through many tests, such as regularly pulling *The Royal Scot* and comfortably going up the Shap incline. They remained in service for an average of fifteen years, and during this time thousands of new steam engines were built. The question has to be, why? It was brilliant for steam enthusiasts but would it have been more sensible to build upgraded versions of Classes D16/1 and D16/2? Perhaps coal was cheaper than oil at the time, or maybe there was a requirement to keep the mines open. Whatever the reason, locomotive footplate men could have been given a much easier steed to work with and a far more comfortable one, despite the many improved Standard classes of steam engines leaving the workshops.

▶ **D132 (brand new) at Derby works in 1961 with D16/2 10203**

Class D16/2 10203 at Derby, with a member of a later generation in the foreground in the form of brand new BR Type 4 Co-Co Class 45 locomotive D132. Seen new in 1962, it would later carry the TOPS (Total Operations Processing System) number 45075. It was built at Crewe Works and introduced in December 1961, being known as Peaks after the first ten locomotives in the original Class 44 that were named after British mountains. It was withdrawn in January 1985 and cut up in October 1986 at Vic Berry of Leicester.

◀ **Peak Class 44 No. D1 Scafell Pike**

Heading towards Acton Bridge station in 1960 is the first member of this small initial class. Just ten were built as Class 44 BR Type 4 Co-Co, and all were named after British mountains. This one, No. D1 *Scafell Pike*, was built in July 1959 at Derby Works and was later given the TOPS number 44001. This class was the precursor of the far larger Classes 45 and 46 and onwards to the new diesel generation. Once the Class 45 locomotives were available to take over the duties of this small class, they all had their steam heating boilers removed and were relegated to goods traffic. D1 was withdrawn in October 1976 and cut up at Derby Works four months later. Only two of the class went into preservation; D4 *Great Gable* was withdrawn in November 1980 and preserved at the Midland Railway at Butterley and D8 *Penyghent* was withdrawn in the same month and went into preservation at Peak Rail, Matlock in Derbyshire.

► EE Type 4 Co-Co Class 40 No. D220

D220 is near the front of this very early class of diesel and was almost new when seen here at Manchester Victoria in the summer of 1959. EE/VF (English Electric/Vulcan Foundry) built it during 1958, and it went into service in July 1959. In February 1963 it was given the name *Franconia* after a Cunard ship, then in February 1974 it was given the TOPS number 40020. It was withdrawn in August 1982 and scrapped at Crewe Works in March 1987.

◄ Deltic Type 5 Co-Co Class 55 No. D9019 *Royal Highland Fusilier*

King's Cross station in 1966, where we see one of the Deltic classes D9019, later Tops 55019 *Royal Highland Fusilier*. It was built at EE/VF in December 1961. It was withdrawn in December 1981 and was one of the lucky ones to go into preservation, having been purchased by the Deltic Preservation Society. Its first base was the North Yorkshire Railway, then the Great Central Railway and the East Lancashire Railway. It is now based at the Deltic Preservation Society site at Barrow Hill. It was the first Deltic Locomotive to be fitted with the TPWS (Train Protection & Warning System).

▲ **Peak Class Type 4 Class 45 1Co-Co1 No. D132**

Another look at a new Peak Class diesel outside the test house of Derby Works in 1962. Built at Crewe Works and delivered in December 1961, it was given the TOPS number 45075 in February 1975 and withdrawn in January 1985. It was cut up by Vic Berry of Leicester in October 1986.

▲ **Class 20 or English Electric Type 1**

A locomotive for which we do not have the number but an interesting shot all the same as a Class 20 diesel-electric locomotive hauls an interesting train of flat wagons and tanks near Hawick, Scotland, circa 1964. One of the wagons is carrying an Austin tractor unit.

◀ **Another Class 20 or EE Type 1**

Another unknown Class 20, this time parked up awaiting its next duty in 1964 at Corker Hill MPD in Glasgow. Class 20 was not the most successful of classes and tended to be used on light goods or double headed.

▼ EE Type 1 Bo-Bo Class 20s Nos D8002/7

Two ex-works locomotives on test heading south at Moore, Near Warrington, circa 1963. Both engines were built at EE/VF in 1957. In September 1974, D8002 received the TOPS number 20002 and D8007 became 20007. D8002 was withdrawn and scrapped in September 1990 at M.C. Metals, Glasgow. D8007 was far luckier as after being withdrawn in 1991 it was purchased by the Churnet Valley Railway, later moving to the Midland Railway Centre at Butterley. It has now been completely overhauled and has been on the rails since 2013.

▲ EE type 4 Class 40 No. D216 *Campania*

It is May 1962 and seen here at Preston station is D216 with a train of maroon carriages, the first one being a parcels van. The engine was built at EE/VF and introduced in June 1959. In the year it was photographed it received the name *Campania*, after a cruise ship, then in November 1973 it received the TOPS number 40016. It was withdrawn in May 1981 and broken up in November 1983 at BREL Swindon.

◄ Inside Derby Workshops in 1966

Work being carried out on a Type 2 Class 24 Bo-Bo diesel D5039. It was built at Crewe works in 1959, going into service in September that year. In June 1974 it was given the TOPS number 24039 and was withdrawn in July 1976 at Crewe, at which time it was put into storage, finally being scrapped at Swindon Works in July 1978.

▼ A new DMU at Derby in 1964

No number is shown, but this is a set of British Rail Derby lightweight diesel multiple units, straight out of the workshops in 1964 and one of the last in the class. It is a class that had been in service from 1954 to 1969 and was a great success as steam was disappearing from the minor lines and multiple units were taking over.

▲ **Hymek B-B Type 1 diesel hydraulic No. D7013**

It is 1967 and one of the least successful of the diesel locomotives, the Beyer Peacock Type 4 B-B Class 35 Hymek hydraulic No. D7013, departs Bristol Temple Meads. The Western Region of BR ordered batches of the class, although head office cancelled a later batch. I think that the suits in Marylebone were in something of a dispute with the Swindon-based GWR Division. Either way, the Hymeks did not last long, this one just under ten years. It was built by Beyer Peacock and went into service in December 1961, being withdrawn in January 1972. It was cut up at Swindon Works in August 1972.

◀ EE Type 4 D383 at Acton Bridge station in 1966

As a result of the 1955 modernisation plan for British Railways it was decided that the West Coast mainline would receive 25kV AC overhead wires. The line between Liverpool Lime Street and Crewe saw the work begin at Lime Street, and then electric services on 1 January 1962. Despite this, diesel traction still used the line, as in this case. D383 from the extensive fleet of 200 Type 4 Co-Co Class 40 engines passes through Acton Bridge. EE/VF built the locomotive and it was released to service in March 1962. In March 1974 it was given the TOPS number 40183, withdrawn from service in June 1983 and scrapped at Crewe Works in June 1986.

▶ BR Derby-Sulzer Type 2 Bo-Bo Class 24 No. D5000

Class leader Class 24 D5000 stood at the head of its train at King's Cross in May 1963. This first in the class was built at Derby works and the engines for the first ten were manufactured in Switzerland by Sulzer Brothers at Winterthur. The locomotive was completed and driven to Marylebone station for inspection by the then Chairman Sir Brian Robertson and his staff. It was then allocated to Crewe South. Note that this engine has a thin stripe at waist level. This is, in fact, painted eggshell blue and was not favoured by the management, so it was the only locomotive in the class to have it. In November 1973 it was given the TOPS number 24005, it was withdrawn from service in January 1976 and cut up at Swindon Works in April 1977.

◄ Diesel mechanical shunter 0-6-0 No. 08646

At the Bulmers cider sidings in Hereford in 1974 we see a ubiquitous shunting engine, many of which are still in use across the country. This can only be expected, as these joint classes contain the most locomotives built in Great Britain. It is a BR diesel-electric 0-6-0, comprising classes 08, 09 and 10. This one had the original number D3813 and had only received its TOPS number 08646 in April 1974. The locomotive was built at Horwich Works and introduced in February 1959. It is still believed to be working in one of the many locations where this class can still be found.

▼ Brush Class 2 Type 2 A1A-A1A No. D5655

King's Cross station in 1967 as the driver of D5655 has a chat with someone, possibly a railway employee. The engine was built by Brush and was introduced in September 1960. In February 1974 it received its TOPS number 31229. Quite a few of this class have been preserved and three are still in service, but D5655/31229 is not one of them.

► **English Electric Type 5 Co-Co Class 55 No. 55018 *Ballymoss***

A hard-working diesel, with the date and location not recorded. No. 55018 was built by EE/VF, introduced in November 1961 and named *Ballymoss* after an Irish racehorse. It was given the number D9018 and received the TOPS number 55018 in February 1974. It was withdrawn on 12 October 1981 and scrapped at BREL Doncaster in January 1982.

▼ **English Electric Type 5 Co-Co Class 55 No. 55016 *Gordon Highlander***

Another hard-working diesel, at an unknown location in 1975. D9016 was built at EE/VF and introduced in October 1961. It received the TOPS number 55016 in February 1974 and was withdrawn in December 1981. However, the story did not end there: it was purchased by the Deltic 9000 fund with the intention of both using it for spares and restoring it. In the early 2000s, it was sent to Porterbrook Leasing and painted purple. In 2008 it was sold to the Harry Needle Railroad Company. Again it was soon sold and in March 2014 it arrived at the Great Central Railway. In December 2016 it was again offered for sale but needing much work.

▲ Peak Class 46 Type 4 Sulzer No. D193

The last locomotive in the class of Sulzer BR Type 4 Co-Co Class 46 heads east through Manchester Victoria station in 1964. It was built at Derby Works and introduced in January 1963 as D193. In November 1970 it was given the TOPS Number 46056 and it was withdrawn in October 1976 from Gateshead, then cut up at Swindon Works in October 1985.

◄ Western Class C-C Type 4 No. D1029 *Western Legionnaire*

Here we have a locomotive that originally had a misspelt name, seen here at Paddington station in early 1967. It was built by BR Swindon and given the name *Western Legionaire*. In September 1967 the fault was discovered and the nameplates were removed, cut in two and then put back together with an extra 'n' inserted to make the correct spelling 'Legionnaire'. This dates the photo as being after the discovery. The driver is having a chat with some trainspotters at the platform end. D1029 was scrapped at BREL Swindon in May 1976.

◄ BRCW Type 3 Bo-Bo Class 33 No. D6542

Seen here at Weymouth motive power depot (MPD) in 1966 is D6542, which was built by the BRCW, introduced in February 1961 and given the TOPS number 33024 in February 1974. It was withdrawn in February 1986 and cut up at BR Eastleigh in May 1986.

▼ Diesel hydraulic Class 52 C-C 4 No. D1056 *Western Sultan*

Shrewsbury MPD in 1964 and another diesel hydraulic member of the BR Type 4 C-C Class 52 stands awaiting its next tour of duty. The class of 74 locomotives was built for the Western Region of BR and this one, *Western Sultan*, was built at Crewe Works and released into service in March 1963. It was withdrawn in December 1976 from Laira and scrapped in May 1979 at Swindon Works.

◄ Brush Type 4 Class 47 Co-Co No. D1654

This locomotive can be seen heading south at Moore in 1967 with a rake of maroon carriages. The locomotive was built at Crewe Works, going into service on 23 January 1965 with the number D1654. In February 1974 it received the TOPS number 47070 and in September 1984 it became 47620 and was named *Windsor Castle* at Paddington Station by HM the Queen. It later became 47835 and was withdrawn from BR Bristol Bath Road on 15 May 1988. In May 1995 it received the number 47799 when in preservation and was named *Prince Henry*. The locomotive was at Eastleigh Works in May 2009.

▼ Class 08 diesel mechanical shunter

A look at the West Coast Mainline running through Acton Bridge station but with an unusual sight: a Class 08 locomotive hauling a freight down it in 1967. Perhaps the steam engine behind it has something to do with it.

▲ **Class 47 No. D1609**

An unusual sight on the main line, especially attached to a train, is a locomotive painted in primer. D1609 is stopped at the signals at Winwick Quay in 1964. This locomotive was built at Crewe Works and taken into service on 11 August 1964, so was probably brand new at this time. In December 1973 it was given the TOPS Number 47030, then became 47618 in August 1984 and 47836 in August 1989. In October 1984 it was given the name *Fair Rosamund*, from 47510. This name was removed in January 1994 when the TOPS number changed again to 47780. The locomotive was withdrawn and scrapped at EMR Kingsbury on 7 August 2007.

▶ **Class 47 No. D1508 and Deltic Class 55 No. D9017** *The Durham Light Infantry*

It's 1967 and seen at King's Cross is D1508, built by Brush in January 1963 and given the TOPS number 47409 in February 1974. It was later named *David Lloyd George* and scrapped at Vic Berry, Leicester, in June 1989. D9017 was built at EE/VF in November 1961 and scrapped at BREL Doncaster in January 1983.

◀ EE Type 4, Co-Co Class 40 No. D324

The last of the Class 40s to be built with disc head code markers as used in steam days. It was decided that trains would instead display the four-character train reporting number. D324 heads south towards Warrington in 1964 with its train of maroon carriages. The locomotive was built by English Electric/Robert Stephenson & Hawthorns Ltd, entering service in June 1961. It received the TOPS number 40124 in February 1974, was withdrawn in January 1984 and was cut up at Doncaster Works in March 1984.

▼ BR Sulzer Type 2 Bo-Bo Class 24 No. D5133

D5133 at an unknown location with a short train in 1967. Built at Derby Works and introduced in October 1960, in February 1974 it was given the TOPS number 24133. It was withdrawn from Crewe in January 1976 and stored. It was finally cut up at Doncaster Works in September 1978.

► **Brush Type 4 Class 47/4 No. D1510 and Deltic Class 55 No. D9013**

What would probably be called a 'good cop' in old trainspotter parlance, seen here at Haymarket in 1964. On the left is Brush Type 4 Class 47/4 D1510, which was built by Brush Traction Loughborough and introduced in February 1963, so it was quite new when seen. It was given the TOPS number 47411 in January 1974 and in May 1987 it was given the name *The Geordie*, which was removed in May 1988. The locomotive was withdrawn in June 1989 and scrapped at BSC Appleby-Frodingham in December 1994.

The second locomotive is English Electric Type 5 Co-Co Class 55 D9013 built by EE/VF and introduced during September 1961. On 16 January 1963, it was named *The Black Watch* during a ceremony at Dundee. In February 1974 it was given the TOPS number 55013 and withdrawn in December 1981. During December 1982 it was cut up at Derby Works.

◄ **BRCW Class 33 No. 33027**

It is 1975 and a BRCW Class 33 is seen here entering Southampton with a passenger train. The locomotive was built by the Birmingham Railway Carriage and Wagon Works and introduced in March 1961. The pre-TOPS number was D6545, and from September 1980 to August 1989 it carried the name *Earl Mountbatten of Burma*, after which the name was transferred to 33207. At the time of writing it is still at work.

▲ A train crash at Acton Grange Junction

On 13 May 1966 EE Type 4 Co-Co D322 was hauling the 20.40 Euston Stranraer Harbour express northbound near Moore. In front of it was the 23.00 Class 8 soda ash train from Northwich to Ravenhead at St Helens. The goods train moved off by the signal and started to climb the gradient. However, the train was loosely coupled, the coupling between the second and third wagons failed, and twenty-nine loaded wagons and the brake van started to roll back. The guard applied the handbrake and jumped clear. The following express continued but at a slow pace and the wagons were also travelling back relatively slowly because of the applied brake. The engine D322 collided with the brake van, and sadly the driver and second man in the cab were killed. None of the passengers were seriously injured. EE/RSH had built the engine and it was introduced in April 1961. It was scrapped in September 1967.

In 1920, when Britain's railways were recovering from the First World War, the multitude of independent railway companies were divided between what became known as 'the Big Four': the LMS (London Midland and Scottish), the GWR (Great Western Railway), the LNER (London and North-Eastern Railway) and the SR (Southern Railway). The biggest of these was the LMS. These companies did their duty for the war effort in the Second World War, in the process the rolling stock and infrastructure becoming worn out through lack of maintenance and overwork. After the war, something needed to be done to bring the network back to at least a pre-war condition.

In 1947 the new Labour government decided to nationalise the railways and other forms of transport, renaming the system as British Railways or BR. This was authorised by the Transport Act 1947 and came into force on 1 January 1948. Initially, the word British Railways could be seen on all locomotives taken into BR or built in the very early days of the new administration. Later, logos including a lion and wheel replaced the words 'British Railways' on all locomotives. Nationalisation was the Labour Party's aim and it included the canals, road haulage/transport and even Thomas Cook travel agents in the mix. Committees were set up to decide on the future of this new government-led railway industry under the auspices of the British Transport Commission (BTC). It was decided to keep the names of 'the Big Four' but as divisions of BR. They mulled over the question of the powertrain for the new locomotives. Should they stick with coal power or look at other things such as diesel and electric?

The decision was made: coal mines provided the coal and employed many miners, while steam engines worked quite well. For the time being, it was decided to stick with coal, but at the same time look at the other forms of power. Some pre-war railway engineers still worked in the industry, and new railway engineers were arriving on the scene. These were men such as George Ivatt, Robert Riddles and the short-lived George Peppercorn, all brilliant engineers. An order was placed for a new breed of standard steam locomotives that would be easier to both maintain and service.

This chapter will look at standard traction brought in after nationalisation, starting with two examples of the stock that was still in use and would join the Standards to work on the new British Railways for the foreseeable future, and hopefully allow the system to make a profit.

▲ Johnson 0-6-0 No. 43282

Only one of two examples in this chapter of a pre-nationalisation locomotive that was brought into British Railways and gave good service for several more years. This Johnson 0-6-0 No. 43282 was built in 1891 by Neilson & Co. and went into service on 13 June. It is seen here with a Belpaire firebox, looking very smart after a works overhaul as it goes about its duties in the Southern shunting yards of Warrington in 1959. It was withdrawn from Warrington Dalam on 13 October 1962 and scrapped at Cashmores of Great Bridge in October 1963 after seventy-one years, ten months and thirteen days.

▲ Jubilee 4-6-0 No. 45690 *Leander*

The second and final pre-nationalisation engine in this chapter is at steam town Carnforth in the winter of 1981, where 45690 is prepared for duties hauling a Santa Special. This Stanier-designed locomotive is seen in pre-nationalisation LMS livery and bearing the number 5690. It was built at Crewe Works, going into service on 9 March 1936 with the name *Leander*, after HMS *Leander*.

It was withdrawn in 1964 and sent to the Barry scrapyard. In 1972, Brian Oliver rescued her and the Leander Locomotive Society restored her at Derby. Starting at Dinting, it did the rounds of the preserved railways until it ended up in possession of Chris Beet of the National Railway Museum, and the West Coast Railway Company now operates her from its Carnforth MPD base.

► **A1 Class 4-6-2 No. 60154**
Bon Accord

It is 1965 at Leeds Neville Hill MPD and with its back to the camera is Peppercorn-designed locomotive 60154 *Bon Accord*. It was built at Doncaster Works and entered service on 24 September 1949. It was withdrawn from Neville Hill on 4 October 1965 and scrapped at T.W. Ward, Beighton, Sheffield, the following month. The name *Bon Accord* comes from the Aberdeen coat of arms.

◄ **Standard Class 5 No. 73096**

Seen at Patricroft MPD in early 1968 is a locomotive that started and finished its working life on BR at this motive power depot. Riddles designed and built it at Derby Works and it went into service in November 1955. It was withdrawn from here on 11 November 1967 and sold for scrap to Woodham Brothers scrapyard in Barry. In 1985 John Bunch, a Hampshire-based businessman at the Mid Hants Railway, rescued the engine and restored it. In 1993 restoration was complete, and it was put back into service on the Mid Hants Railway/The Watercress Line. In 2009 the engine suffered £200,000 worth of damage but it was repaired and returned to service the following year. In September 2011 the boiler certificate expired and the engine was taken to the Southall Railway Centre, where it was stored. In 2015, it was purchased from John Bunch by the Mid Hants Railway Plc and is awaiting a major overhaul there.

▲ **Two BR Standard Class 5MTs 4-6-0s Nos 73050 and 73125**

A pair of Riddles Standard Class 5s, complete with hand-drawn smokebox numbers, standing at Patricroft MPD in 1966. The first one, 73050, was built at Derby Works and released into service at Bath Green Park during April 1954. It was withdrawn from Patricroft in June 1968. That same year the Rev. Richard Patten purchased it for the scrap value of £3,000 with the intention of displaying it outside Peterborough Technology College. The locomotive, however, was found to be in excellent condition, so would have been wasted as a static exhibit. In 1969 the Peterborough branch of the East

Anglian Locomotive Society was launched with the intention of buying 70000 *Britannia*. After much change, the Nene Valley Railway was born with 73050 as one of its stars. It has now been named the *City of Peterborough* and at the time of writing is undergoing a heavy overhaul at Wanstead.

The second loco, 5MT 73125, is one of the classes with Caprotti valve gear. It was built at Derby Works, going into service in July 1956 at Shrewsbury. It was withdrawn from this MPD in June 1968 and cut up at Cashmores of Great Bridge four months later.

► Britannia Class 4-6-2 No. 70012 *John of Gaunt*

No. 70012 heads south towards Warrington at Moore Lane in 1966. This Riddles-designed locomotive was built at Crewe Works in May 1951 and allocated to Norwich Thorpe. It was withdrawn from Carlisle Kingmoor on 30 December 1967 and scrapped at T.W. Ward, Killamarsh, three months later.

▼ Metrovick Co-Bo Type 2 and Class 28 No. D5714

At Leyland in Lancashire in 1963, heading south with a passenger train, is a Metrovick Class 28 D5714. It was built by Metropolitan-Vickers in April 1959 with a unique wheel arrangement Co-Bo, meaning a six-wheel bogie at one end and a four-wheel one at the other. It was withdrawn in September 1968 and scrapped at J. Cashmore, Great Bridge, the following September. Not one of BR's big success stories, the Crossley eight-cylinder engines were prone to problems. The locomotive was only in service for nine years, and one of them was in storage.

◄ **BR/EE Class 86 No. 86013,** *later County of Lancashire*

Two locomotives of the Class 86 seen ex-works at Wilmslow station in 1976. The first one has the number 86013 and was built at BR Doncaster. An early member of this massive class, it was introduced in November 1965 with the number E3128. In August 1973 it received the TOPS number 86013, which in 1989 changed to 86413, then finally 86613. In April 1985 it received the name *County of Lancashire*. Many have now been scrapped and some exported to Bulgaria and Hungary. At the time of writing it is still in service.

▼ **Brush Type 4 Bo-Bo Class 4748 No. D1607**

An excellent view of a quite new Class 47 at Shrewsbury MPD in 1965. It was built at BR Crewe and released into service in July 1964, with its first MPD being Swansea Landore. In April 1974 it received the TOPS number 47477. It was withdrawn on 28 October 1992 and scrapped at Booth-Row Metals, Rotherham, in July 1993.

▲ **Standard Class 9F 2-10-0 92157**

Another of the powerful but short-lived Riddles 9F Standard Class Locomotives, at Edge Hill MPD in Liverpool during 1966. No. 92157 was built at Crewe Works and released into service at Saltley on 31 July 1957.

It was withdrawn from Carlisle Kingmoor In September 1967 and scrapped at Motherwell Machinery and Scrap the following February.

As the 1950s progressed, it was time to look at the state of the railways. The Conservatives had already dumped some of the more outlandish nationalisations but the railways were still losing money. In 1955 the government introduced the Modernisation Plan, or to give it its full title, 'Modernisation and Re-Equipment of the British Railways'. The government made a loan to the BTC of up to £250 million (almost £2 billion in 2019), with a rider that it had to be paid back at a proper rate of interest based on the toughest commercial considerations. In retrospect, it was an abject failure. One of the prompts for this plan was a recent strike by footplatemen that brought the country to its knees. One of the problems was gross overstaffing, mainly due to steam traction both on the footplate and off it, so it was time to cut back.

Some parts of the plan worked, but some were silly. The electrification of some main lines and the withdrawal of steam in favour of diesel was a rather obvious answer. As an interim measure capital was wasted on new marshalling yards and steam facilities that were soon obsolete. Containerisation was increased and became the norm, and many yards were scrapped prematurely. A massive order for new diesel locomotives was made both in railway workshops and with private builders, but the introduction of untried and hardly tested diesel and electrics contracted out to an assortment of building companies was another mistake. During this period there were many breakdowns, and steam traction often had to come to the rescue. The building of steam locomotives also continued, and the British Transport Commission had already overseen the closure of many miles of branch lines.

However, the takings year by year were never enough. The BTC Report for 1961 shows that during 1960 British Railways had a deficit of £67.7 million, whereas in 1959 it had only been £42 million. The deficit for all nationalised undertakings was £100.9 million. It couldn't go on. But more was to come when the Minister of Transport, Ernest Marples, brought in Dr Richard Beeching to continue the cuts. At the time, it seemed like a good idea, but in retrospect it was very short-sighted. The plan did not work!

This next chapter will be dedicated to looking at the rail network through these years when steam and other forms of power worked together on British railways.

▲ **EE Type 4 Co-Co Class 40 No. D390**

Standing outside Patricroft MPD is a Class 4 Diesel D390, while behind it and in steam, is a BR Standard 4-6-0 without smokebox number plate. The diesel was built at EE/VF and introduced in May 1962. It was withdrawn in January 1976 and cut up at BREL Crewe in April 1976.

▲ **9F 2-10-0 No. 92208 and** *Metro Vickers Co-Bo* **No. D5700**

Straight out of the paint shop at Crewe Works in 1965, when the works were open to the public, is a Riddles-designed 9F with no number plate but looking good nonetheless. It was built at Swindon Works during June 1959 and allocated to Plymouth Laira. It was withdrawn from Carlisle Kingmoor on 31 October 1967 at the ripe old age of eight years. Just what was BR thinking of at the time? It was cut up at J. McWilliams of Shettleston four months later. The diesel at the side is Metro Vickers Co-Bo No. D5700, the class leader of Class 28. It was introduced in July 1958 and withdrawn in December 1967 to be cut up at J. McWilliam, Shettleston. A Dapol N Gauge model of the engine has been preserved to keep its memory alive.

◀ **EE Type 4 No. D235 *Apapa* and Black 5 4-6-0 No. 44865**

EE Type 4 Diesel D235 heads south with a passenger train at Leyland, south of Preston, in 1967. The locomotive was built by EE/VF and entered service in October 1959. In 1962 it was given the name *Apapa*, then in February 1974 it was given the TOPS number 40035. It was withdrawn in September 1984 and scrapped at Crewe Works in June 1985. The Stanier Black 5 44865 sitting light engine at the signals was built at Crewe Works during February 1945 and in 1949 it was allocated to Crewe North. It was withdrawn from Crewe South on 30 September 1967 and scrapped at Cashmores of Great Bridge three months later.

◄ **Clayton Bo-Bo Class 17 D8550 and a Black Five 4-6-0 No. 44850**

Our mix of propulsion here gives us what is reputed to be the least successful diesel locomotive and a Black Five that is one of the most respected steam engines on BR. They sat together at Corkerhill, Glasgow, in 1964. The driver of the diesel is climbing on to D8550. Clayton built the locomotive and introduced it in November 1962; it was withdrawn in October 1971 and scrapped at Cashmores of Great Bridge in September 1975. The Stanier Black Five 4-6-0 44850 was built at Crewe Works during November 1944, and it was withdrawn from Motherwell on 31 July 1966. Two months later it was scrapped at Motherwell Machinery and Scrap.

▲ **Black Five 4-6-0 No. 45080 and Co-Co Class 47 No. D1635**

Another engine straight from the paint shop during the 1965 open day at Crewe Works is Black Five 45080. It was built at the Vulcan Foundry in March 1935, withdrawn from Leeds Holbeck on 31 October 1967 and scrapped at T.W. Ward at Killamarsh four months later. Also present is Brush Type 4 Co-Co Class 47 No. D1635, which received the TOPS number 47053 in March 1974. It was built at Crewe Works and introduced in December 1964. For some of its life it carried the name *Elland,* and it has now been withdrawn. The Metrovick D5700 at the front has been detailed earlier.

▼ Western 4CC Type 4 Class 52 No. D1050 *Western Ruler* and Collett 4-6-0 6876 *Kingsland Grange*

The driver of the quite new D1050 *Western Ruler* looks back along his locomotive at Shrewsbury MPD in 1963. The BR Western Region discovered that the Warships and Hymeks did not have the power required, hence the order for a Class 52 that would fill the requirement for more power. They did the job but could have been better. They also had to compete later with the new electrics and high-speed trains, so they had a relatively short lifespan. D1050 was built at Crewe Works and introduced in January 1963 named *Western Ruler*. It was withdrawn in April 1975 and scrapped at Swindon Works in April 1976. Charles Collett designed the steam engine shown, 6876 *Kingsland Grange*, and it was built at Swindon Works for the GWR during April 1939. In 1948 it was allocated to St Philips Marsh, withdrawn from Worcester on 30 November 1965 and scrapped at Cashmores of Newport two months later.

▲ 4-6-0 Black Five 44729 and Cravens multiple unit sets

At Manchester Victoria in 1962 and a Cravens multiple unit is at the platform as two trainspotters mark down the numbers – one using his knee as a desk! On the opposite platform at the head of a train is Stanier Black Five 44729, which was built at Crewe Works during January 1949 and on nationalisation could be found at Stockport Edgeley. It was withdrawn on 31 October 1966 and scrapped at Drapers Neptune Street Goods Yard on 28 February 1967.

▶ Western Class CC Type 4 and Hall Class 4-6-0 No. 5933 *Kingsway Hall*

A perfect example of mixed traffic during the transition from steam to diesel and electric is this scene at Paddington station. The date is May 1963 as the two engines stand together, the maroon Western and ethereal Hall Class being *Kingsway Hall*. The number of the Western is not known, but Collett-designed 5933 was built at Swindon Works during June 1933. It was withdrawn from Oxford on 31 August 1965 and scrapped at Birds of Bynea three months later.

▲ **Standard Class 9F 2-10-0 No. 92139**

Half in, half out of Leeds Holbeck MPD in 1965 is another Standard Class 9F, 92139. The Riddles-designed locomotive was built at Crewe Works and went into service on 21 July 1957 at Saltley. It was withdrawn from Carlisle Kingmoor in September 1967 and scrapped at Motherwell Machinery and Scrap the following February.

▼ Beyer Peacock Hymek Type 3 B-B Class 35 No. D7079 and 4-6-2 No. 34102 West Country Class *Lapford*

Another look at a relatively unsuccessful diesel locomotive and a successful steam engine at Weymouth MPD in 1965. The Hymek built by Beyer Peacock and introduced in December 1963 was withdrawn in October 1971 and scrapped at Swindon Works in August 1972. The Bulleid-designed

West Country Class 34102 *Lapford* was built during March 1950. It was withdrawn on 31 July 1967 from Eastleigh and scrapped in September 1968 at Cashmores of Newport. This made it the last un-rebuilt member of the West Country Class to be withdrawn.

▲ **Birmingham RCW three-car sets and 8F No. 48723**

A scene well remembered from the late 1950s and '60s is this scene between Leyland and Preston in 1967. A train of two three-car DMU sets of Birmingham Carriage and Wagon Works stock passes a Stanier 8F in the opposite direction.

No. 48723 was built at Brighton Works in August 1944. It was withdrawn from Lostock Hall on the very last day of regular steam working, 3 August 1968, and was scrapped at T.W. Ward of Beighton the following December.

◀ **EE Type 4 Co-Co Class 50 No. D420**

D420 heads south out of Preston and passes an unknown Black Five in early 1968. EE/VF built the diesel and introduced it into service in May 1968. In February 1974 it was given the TOPS number 50020, then in July 1978 it was given the name *Revenge* to commemorate a Royal Navy nuclear submarine. It was withdrawn on 27 July 1990 and scrapped at Booth Rowe Scrapyard in June 1992.

▶ **Jubilee Class 4-6-0 No. 45589 Gwalior**

A two-car DMU heading for Crewe near Warrington Bank Quay station passes 45589 going in the opposite direction in 1962. The North British Locomotive Company built the Jubilee in Glasgow and it entered service on 15 December 1934. It was withdrawn on 22 March 1965 from Wakefield and scrapped at Cashmores of Great Bridge a year later.

A DECISION IS MADE: STICK WITH STEAM FOR THE TIME BEING

As the 1950s progressed, the nationalised British Railways continued to build new steam locomotives and tried out different types of diesel. Some were a success, but many were not. The Hymeks and hydraulic locomotives left a lot to be desired and had frequent breakdowns. There were very successful classes such as the 47s, but it was an era when the BTC wanted to save money and was not doing so. Massive orders for new, untried diesels proved expensive and indicated poor management of the system. In the meantime, the steam locomotive continued to work hard, a fact not lost on railway enthusiasts. However, Beeching had not yet arrived on the scene, so for this chapter we will stick with steam traction and enjoy a look at what would soon be ending on the mainline revenue-earning services.

◀ Royal Scot Class 4-6-0 No. 46115 *Scots Guardsman*

Scots Guardsman is seen here on an RCTS (Railway Correspondence and Travel Society) rail tour at Hellifield station on 13 February 1965. Even before steam was banned there were classic rail tours, and the RCTS was one of the most active groups, then as now. *Scots Guardsman* was built at the North British Locomotive Company in Glasgow, going into service in October 1927, originally with a Fowler-designed parallel boiler. Between 1943 and 1955 the whole class was substantially rebuilt to the plans of William Stanier, including the fitting of tapered boilers. It was withdrawn on 1 January 1961. Its first claim to fame was its part as the engine in the well-known 1936 film *Night Mail* (together with unnamed Patriot

No. 45513). At withdrawal, it was one of only two Royal Scots to be preserved, and it ended up at the Keighley and Worth Valley Railway. It was decided that at that time it was too large and was delivered to the Dinting Railway Centre. It remained there until it was taken to the Birmingham Railway Museum at Tylsley in 1989 for an overhaul. This did not happen, so eventually it was bought by David Smith, the owner of the West Coast Railway Company, and by 2008 it was back to mainline standard. In 2012 *Flying Scotsman* was due to convey the Olympic Torch from York to Shildon but when the engine failed *Scots Guardsman* undertook the duty. At the time of writing, it is undergoing an overhaul.

▲ Unknown Britannia 4-6-2

An unnamed, Riddles-designed Britannia Class engine at Eastleigh in 1965, the period charm of the classic and suitably battered British Rail

truck matching the battered and nameless, once pride of the rails, Britannia engine.

▼ **Warship-Class diesel hydraulic B-B Class 43 Type 4**

An enthusiast photographs a Class 43 as it enters Salisbury station in 1966. Unfortunately, there is no name or number on this occasion, but it is nonetheless an example of the change in motive power in the days preceding the end of steam. This class was based upon the V200 class of German diesel hydraulics and built between 1960 and 1962.

▲ **Black 5 4-6-0 No. 45052, 8F 2-8-0 No. 48431 and an Ivatt 2-6-2T**

A typical photograph of a busy steam MPD, in this case Stockport Edgeley in 1966. The frontmost locomotive on view is a Black Five 45052 that was built at the Vulcan Foundry in November 1934. At nationalisation it was at Rugby, and it was withdrawn from Crewe South on 30 September 1967 to be scrapped at Cashmores, Great Bridge, in March 1968. There are no details of the far engine other than it is an Ivatt 2-6-2.

The engine next to 45052 is 8F 2-8-0 48431 with a snow plough. It was built at Swindon Works, going into service on 11 March 1944. It

was withdrawn on 6 May 1964 from Bath Green Park. It is one of the lucky 'Consuls', as enthusiasts called the class, as it was sent for scrap to Woodhams scrapyard at Barry. It remained there until 1972, when it was rescued by the Keighley and Worth Valley Railway (KWVR). After much hard work, the locomotive was back on the rails in December 1975. It now needs a further restoration and for the time being is a static exhibit at the Oxenhope Exhibition Shed on the KWVR.

◄ **Stanier Black Five Class 4-6-0 No. 44668 and an 8F 2-8-0**

Staying at Stockport Edgeley MPD in 1966 and there is a Stanier Black Five 4-6-0 with an unknown 8F. The Black Five was built at Horwich Works during December 1949. It was withdrawn from Carlisle Kingmoor on 30 April 1966 and scrapped at Motherwell Machinery and Scrap at Inslow Works, Wishaw.

▼ **Jubilee Class 4-6-0 No. 45574 *India***

In this panoramic view of railway sidings we see Jubilee 45574 *India* as it shunts the carriage sidings north of Manchester Victoria station in 1964. It is also an example of just how abused steam engines were as the end drew near. *India* was built at the North British Locomotive Company, Glasgow, in September 1934 and on nationalisation could be found at Blackpool Central. It was withdrawn from Leeds Holbeck on 31 March 1966 and scrapped at Drapers, Neptune Street Goods Yard, Hull, during August 1966.

▲ **Gresley Class A4 4-6-2 No. 60019 *Bittern***

Steam traction was already in demand for rail tours before steam ended. In this case, 60019 *Bittern* is at Derby station on a Williams Deacons Bank Railtour on 6 March 1966. The locomotive was built at Doncaster Works in December 1937 and given the LNER number 4464, changed in 1946 to 60019. In 1948 it was at Aberdeen Ferryhill. On 5 September 1966, it was withdrawn and sold to Geoff Drury seven days later. The engine was in quite a poor state and BR omitted to mention that, among other things, its frames were cracked quite badly. It operated from what is now the York Railway Museum site but soon had to be laid up. Geoff Drury then purchased Peppercorn Class A2 60532 *Blue Peter*, and it and *Bittern* were moved to the Dinting Railway Centre near Glossop. Neither engine was used much and in late 1987 they went on long-term loan to the North Eastern Locomotive Preservation Group (NELPG). In 2013 *Bittern* broke the speed record for a preserved steam locomotive. At the time of writing *Bittern* is queuing up for workshop space to become available at Crewe Locomotive Services Ltd for a refit.

▼ Jubilee Class 4-6-0 No. 45632 *Tonga*

No. 45632 seen here in 1964 on Dallam MPD at Warrington, to the left is rebuilt Patriot 4-6-0 No. 45531 *Sir Frederick Harrison*. *Tonga* bears the yellow stripe on the cab that denotes its inability to go further south than Crewe station. It was built at Crewe Works in November 1934 and in 1953 was allocated to Longsight in Manchester. It was withdrawn from Newton Heath in October 1965 and scrapped at Cashmores, Great Bridge, in May 1966. Rebuilt 4-6-0 Patriot Class 45531 *Sir Frederick Harrison* was built at Crewe

Works, going into service on 7 April 1933. It was withdrawn from Carlisle Kingmore on 30 October 1965 and scrapped at Campbells of Airdrie. The name was given to commemorate Sir Frederick Harrison (1844–1914) who rose from a clerk at Shrewsbury on the LNWR, then became a lieutenant colonel in the Engineer and Railway Staff Corps. He was knighted in 1902 as a senior officer with the South Eastern & Chatham Railway Companies Joint Management Committee.

► Jubilee Class 4-6-0 No. 45732 *Sanspareil*

Here we have another member of the extensive Stanier Jubilee Class seen with a train of coal wagons at Preston station in 1962. The engine was built at Crewe Works, going into service on 29 October 1936. It was withdrawn

from Stockport Edgeley in February 1964 and cut up by G.W. Butler at Otley six months later. (*Sans Pareil* was a locomotive that took part in the 1829 Rainhill trials.)

▲ BR 'open day' circa 1962 at Manchester Central station

Manchester Central was a mainline terminus at Manchester from 1880 to 1969. It was built by the Cheshire Lines Committee (CLC) and designed by Sir John Fowler. The Greater Manchester Exhibition Centre, or G-Mex Centre, was opened by the Queen in 1986 after four years of renovation. It is now Manchester Central Conference Centre and a Grade II listed building. At an open day in 1962 the main attraction is Coronation Class 4-6-2 45256 *Sir William A Stanier FRS*, the second to last of the Coronation class built and named for the designer. Also among the treats on view is Class 11F Improved Director Class 4-4-0 506 *Butler Henderson* and Midland Railway 1000 Class 4-4-0 1000. Also present were other steam locomotives, together with diesel and electric. The openness of the freedom given to enthusiasts in those days would not apply today. As can be seen, health and safety was of secondary importance to having a good time on the exhibits.

The exhibits include one that should have been top of the list for preservation but slipped through the net, No. 46256 *Sir William A Stanier FRS*. It was built in December 1947 under George Ivatt, using some of his updating such as the use of roller bearings. It was second to last in the class, the last being the *City of Salford* built the following year and, again, not preserved. No. 46257 was withdrawn on 31 October 1964 and scrapped at Cashmores, Great Bridge, just two months later.

No. 506 *Butler Henderson* was designed by J.G. Henderson as the prototype for the class and was built at Gorton Works Manchester in 1920 for the Great Central Railway. It was named after Captain the Honourable Eric Brand Butler-Henderson (1884–1953), who was the last director of the Great Central Railway in 1918. The locomotive entered BR on amalgamation and was withdrawn in 1960 to be taken into preservation for the National Collection. It was restored for use on the main line, but when its boiler certificate expired in 1992 it became a static exhibit at the National Railway Museum, York.

Midland Railway 1000 Class 4-4-0 1000 was designed by S.W. Johnson and built at Derby Works in 1902. This was the first locomotive designed by Johnson, and he used the three-cylinder compound arrangement alongside the Smith system, which utilised Smith's starting arrangement. Richard Deeley later upgraded the locomotive, modifying the design for use by later members of the class. Nos 1000 to 1004 became Deeley Compounds with the title Smith/Johnson. From number 1005 onwards they were called simply Deeley Compounds. No. 1000 was prepared for preservation and in 1958 it was restored as near as possible to its 1907 Midland Railway condition. At the time of writing, it is still in the National Collection and on loan to the Barrow Hill Engine Shed in Derbyshire.

▼ Jubilee Class 4-6-0 No. 45663 *Jervis*

Seen heading North at Winwick Junction with a mixed freight in 1963 is another of William Stanier's excellent Jubilee Class, No. 45663 *Jervis*. The locomotive was built in August 1934 at the North British Locomotive Company, Glasgow. In 1948 it was at Carlisle Upperby, and it was withdrawn from Warrington Dallam on 27 November 1965 and cut up at Cashmores of Great Bridge five months later.

◄ Darlington works visit on 3 October 1964

The engine in the foreground is Edward Thompson-designed LNER B1 4-6-0 No. 61330. It was built at the North British Locomotive Company, Glasgow, and went into service at New England on 23 June 1948. It was withdrawn from Thornton Junction on 19 November 1966 and scrapped the following month at Motherwell Machinery and Scrap, Wishaw.

▲ Darlington works visit, 3 October 1964

The nearest locomotive is Q6 0-8-0 63393, built during October 1913 at this workshop and designed by Sir Vincent Litchfield Raven to an NE design. It was withdrawn on 30 June 1964 and scrapped at this works four months later. A 7mm 'O' Scale model was made by D.J.H. Model Loco (D.J.H. Engineering Ltd).

The furthest locomotive is BR Standard 4 2-6-0 76020. This Riddles-designed Standard was built at this works in December 1952 and allocated here. Its last shed was Chester, from where it was withdrawn in April 1966 and scrapped three months later at Birds of Long Marston.

▲ Jubilee Class 4-6-0 No. 45590
Travancore

Heading with a freight northbound through Warrington in 1963 is another Jubilee. It was built at the North British Locomotive Works at Glasgow during December 1934 and allocated on amalgamation to Sheffield Millhouses. Its last shed was Warrington Dallam, from where it was withdrawn on 11 December 1965 and scrapped at Cashmores of Great Bridge three months later. In 1959 *Travancore* came to grief when the driver backed on to the turntable at Kentish Town when it was facing the other way, putting the tender in the pit!

◄ Fairburn 4P 2-6-4 tank No. 42297

A visit to Edge Hill MPD in Liverpool in 1966 and a Charles Fairburn-designed 2-6-4 tank is simmering gently awaiting its next duty. It was built at Derby and entered service on 1 December 1947. It was withdrawn from Lostock Hall on 6 May 1967 and scrapped at Cashmores of Great Bridge four months later.

▼ Black Five 4-6-0 No. 45037

The driver and fireman of Stanier Black Five 45037 lean out to watch the photographer, Phil, in action at Acton Bridge station in 1966. The loco is attached to a passenger train that will be travelling north on the West Coast Main Line.

It was built at the Vulcan Foundry during September 1934 and in 1948 could be found at Patricroft. It was withdrawn from Stoke on 30 November 1965 and scrapped two months later at Cashmores of Great Bridge.

Let us enjoy some more of what is now classic steam traction, but at the time was just plain old steam engines going about their duties. These were locomotives in various schemes, enthralling trainspotters, boys, and some girls; who now prefer the name enthusiasts. Unfortunately, the term 'trainspotting' has, thanks to hip comedians with anorak jokes and films about drug taking, become somewhat derogatory. But for the generation who were happy to be called trainspotters in those innocent and halcyon days, the hobby induces many happy memories. They were not sitting playing computer games but out in the fresh air, travelling around enjoying the thrill of copping a rare cop and filling their Ian Allan ABCs. They were visiting engine sheds and breathing in the warm smells of smoke, oil and, well, steam engines. Now and again they would 'bunk' into a shed to get close up to the occupants, though certainly not to 'tag' one with spray paint or damage anything.

In the next two chapters we will look at more modern traction and then the lucky engines that have been preserved. In the meantime, enjoy some more period steam engines. Due to this being near to the demise of mainline steam, the cleanliness of the locos perhaps leaves a bit to be desired, but the last chapter shows how they used to appear in the good old days with a look at our preserved stock.

◀ Jubilee Class 4-6-0 No. 45664 *Nelson*

At Winwick Junction 45664 *Nelson* heads south towards Warrington in 1963. The tail end of the goods train it is passing gives a view of the guard peering from his bay window. Those windows were provided to enable the guard to see down each side of his train, and apart from seeing Phil taking his photo he is using the window for the purpose it was provided. No. 45664 *Nelson* was built at Derby Works during January 1935 and on amalgamation was at Trafford Park. It was withdrawn from Warrington Dallam on 31 May 1965 and scrapped two months later at Drapers Neptune Street Goods Yard, Hull.

▲ Black Five 4-6-0 No. 45298

It is 1963, and this passenger train hauled by Black Five 45298 is stopped at the signals on the girder bridge over the Mersey heading south of Warrington. The engine is fitted with a self-weighing tender. It was built at Armstrong Whitworth for the LMS, going into service in December 1937. It was withdrawn from Crewe South in September 1967 and scrapped at Cohens of Kettering five months later.

◄ Black Five 4-6-0 No. 45083 and an 8F 2-8-0

On the Chester line at Moore in 1962, what is about to occur in trainspotting terms is a 'blackout', which is when two trains pass, making the details of one of them impossible to see. The Black Five was built at the Vulcan Foundry during March 1935. It was withdrawn from Newton Heath on 31 December 1967 and scrapped at Drapers Neptune Street Goods yard five months later.

▼ Hall Class 4-6-0 No. 7920 *Coney Hall* and 8F No. 48691

On shed at Shrewsbury MPD in 1963 is Hawksworth-designed GWR engine 7920 *Coney Hall* alongside 8F 48691. *Coney Hall* was built at Swindon Works in September 1950 and allocated to Gloucester Horton Road. It was withdrawn from Worcester on 30 June 1965 and scrapped at Cohens, Morriston, Swansea, three months later. The 8F was built at Brighton Works in 1944 and withdrawn from Newton Heath on 19 March 1966, to be scrapped three months later at Cashmores Great Bridge.

► Black Five 4-6-0 No. 44741

No. 44741 heads a mixed freight towards Chester at Moore Lane in 1962. The engine was built at Crewe Works and went into service on 12 June 1948 as one of the last of its class. It was withdrawn on 31 March 1965 and scrapped eight months later at Cashmores of Great Bridge.

▼ Crab Mogul 2-6-0 No. 42783

This Hughes-designed engine heads a car-train northbound through Warrington station in 1962. The engines in the class were nicknamed Horwich Crabs, but this one was built at Crewe Works in September 1927. It was withdrawn from Birkenhead on 14 August 1965 for scrapping at Birds of Long Marston in March 1966.

◄ Black Five 4-6-0 No. 45081

Acting as Warrington station pilot for the day in 1964 is Black Five 45081, which is fitted with a self-weighing tender. The driver and fireman watch as Phil photographs their steed. The engine was built at the Vulcan Foundry during March 1935. It was withdrawn from Carlisle Upperby on 31 October 1965 and scrapped five months later at Campbells of Airdrie.

▼ Unnamed Patriot Class 4-6-0 No. 45508

Here we have quite a rare engine, an unnamed and un-rebuilt Fowler-designed Patriot with a stovepipe chimney. It is double heading with a Black Five 4-6-0 as it heads north over the Mersey bridge towards Warrington in 1960. No. 45508 was built at Crewe Works in August 1932. It was withdrawn from Carlisle Upperby on 3 December 1960 and cut up at Crewe Works three days later. The stovepipe chimney had been fitted in 1956. No members of the class were preserved but a new one, 45551 *The Unknown Warrior*, is under construction at the time of writing.

▼ 8F 2-8-0 No. 48773

No. 48773, seen at Bridgnorth, is a locomotive that has a story to tell and was later preserved. The full story can be found in Chapter 12.

▲ **Coronation Class No. 46229** *Duchess of Hamilton*

One of the preserved Coronation Class LMS Pacific locomotives, *Duchess of Hamilton*, pulling the Limited Edition York/Leeds Railtour on 3 May 1980. It has an attractive and interesting rake of coaches, especially the first one. The locomotive was built in streamlined guise in September 1938 at Crewe Works. The last shed was Edge Hill, from where it was withdrawn on 29 February 1964. It was then purchased with 46233 *Duchess of Sutherland* by Sir Billy Butlin to be a showpiece at his holiday camps. In

the case of 46229, it was sent to Minehead. (The only other preserved Coronation was 46235 *City of Birmingham*, which was presented to Birmingham City Council.) *Duchess of Hamilton* remained at the camp until 1975. The locomotive was donated to the Friends of the NRM at York on a twenty-year loan and purchased by it in 1987. It was soon decided to replace the streamlining and it now stands in the museum in all its original glory. There are plans, however, to return it to the metals.

The original stock that took over from steam on the light traffic lines were diesel rail multiple units. The idea of railcars was not a new one and was first experimented with at the dawn of the railway using steam, but it was not very successful and soon push and pull steam engines were used for the lighter work. Through the years, experiments continued with multiple units powered by steam, diesel and electric, probably the most famous being the GWR diesel railcars that performed good service on the many GWR minor lines. Sentinel-Cammell had success with its steam railcar, and of course there were others, such as the Liverpool Overhead and the London Tube.

We are looking here though at the 1950s and '60s, when steam engines were being culled at a faster and faster rate. Before the Beeching cuts had started to bite, closing lines and stations, there was a requirement for light trains. On the scene came green diesel multiple units, initially with what was called 'cat's whisker' stripes on the front, while later in the interest of safety came yellow panels and full yellow fronts.

Later, full trains of multiple unit stock took over from independent locomotives, the Pendolinos being a good example, and we will look at them later. So here we have a short look at some of the early DMUs that took the work on minor lines from small classes of steam engines.

▶ Manchester to Crewe EMU

At Wilmslow station in 1976.

◀ A set of BR 108 DMU Derby Lightweights

Derby Lightweights clearly showing the 'Cat's Whisker', on the former LNWR line from Lymm to Warrington in 1960. At this time the drivers were happy to leave the blinds behind them open so that passengers in the front seats had a driver's view of the track ahead. Later, they tended to close them, and later still their cabins were blocked off.

▼ A4 car EMU set No. 7816

Forward in time a little now as we visit Southampton in 1975, and arriving under the magnificent signal gantry at Southampton station is an A4 electrical multiple unit. The shot is complemented by the sight of a small group of enthusiasts, books in hand, which includes a girl.

▲ **A two-car set of Derby 'Bed Pan' Lightweights**

A two-car set of Derby Lightweight DMUs depart Earlstown for Liverpool in May 1980. The view highlights the railway network in the days after the end of steam and before privatisation.

▶ **Night-time EMU set at Crewe station**

This EMU is probably on the Crewe Liverpool service and provides another example of the atmosphere at Crewe overnight, in this case, the rain has added to the ambience. The class was very common at the time, circa 1968, but most have now gone to the great scrapyard in the sky.

▲ **A Derby lightweight and two Craven three-car sets of DMUs**

Derby Midland station in 1962.

◄ **Metro Cammell DMU three-car set**

The location is not known in this scene taken in 1976, but the Metro Cammell DMU is an early model that will soon be at the end of its service.

▲ A three-car set of Craven DMUs at Hereford in 1976.

▲ **Two sets of Type 503 EMUs, lead set M28383M, tail set M79187M**

Seen at Neston Dee Junction towards Neston station in 1964 is one of the Wirral electric units that is powered by a 650v DC third rail. The 503 Class was built in two batches, first in 1938 for the LMS and then a second for BR in 1956.

◄ **Class 108 two-car set of DMUs**

The 'cat's whisker' front ends have now given way to yellow panels on these DMUs. They were built by the Birmingham Railway Carriage and Wagon Company and this one is seen at Crewe station in 1963.

▼ Class 142 No. 142012 (Pacer)

On the Chester Manchester line approaching east towards Northwich in 2016. This is a former First North Western facelifted unit that was built by BREL Derby in conjunction with Leyland, which provided the Leyland National bus parts and the Leyland bus four-wheeled underframes. It was built between 1985 and 1987 and is still in service and operated by DB Cargo, late DB Shenker Rail UK and before that English Welsh and Scottish Railway (EWS).

▲ **Class 325 EMU No. 325005** *The Royal Mail Train*

Passing through Acton Bridge station and heading north in 2017 is a Class 325 Mail Train. This is a member of a small class of postal units based on Class 319s and built by ABB (Asea Brown-Boveri) Derby, which purchased the Derby Locomotive Works. The company went on to be owned by Adtranz and then Bombardier Transportation. This class was built between 1995 and 1996 as dedicated Royal Mail EMUs. Sixteen sets were built, and one has been scrapped. The operators are DB Cargo.

◄ Deltic DP1 (Diesel Prototype No. 1)

Pictured here is the precursor to all the Deltics that were to follow, the prototype DP1, better known as the Blue Deltic. In 1943 the Admiralty investigated the development of an engine to be used in its motor torpedo boats. It was to be a lightweight diesel engine and the company Napier already had experience in designing diesel-powered aero engines in conjunction with the German company Junkers. As a result, the Admiralty gave the contract to Napier's parent company, English Electric. Over the years Deltic Engines became the favoured power plant for smaller naval vessels. So when seeking out an engine for the prototype DPI, Deltic was the favoured option. This prototype was built by English Electric at its Dick Kerr Plant at Preston in 1955 with a power plant of two Napier Deltic engines. Although called DP1, it had the project title 'Enterprise' and it was to be named as such. However, Hudswell Clarke beat them to it, giving its range of small diesel locomotives this name. It was painted blue with the large Deltic name along the side, and the name stuck for the following classes of Deltic diesel.

Two engines were fitted, the same as those used in minesweepers although they were derated from 1,750hp to 1,600hp. The locomotive went into service in 1955 on the West Coast Mainline hauling goods trains, and later the named expresses such as 'The Shamrock' and 'The Merseyside Express'. It was withdrawn in March 1961 and can now be found in the National Railway Museum at Shildon.

► EE Class 20 (brand new)

The number cannot be made out here, but the locomotive is brand new and straight out of Vulcan Foundry, VF/EE. It is seen here heading south at Winwick circa 1963.

◄ Class 03 073 diesel shunter

Diesel shunter 03 073 at the Crewe Heritage Centre on 6 June 2018. It was built as D2073 at Doncaster Works during November 1959 and withdrawn on 23 May 1989. On 6 August 1992 it was taken to the Railway Age/Heritage Centre at Crewe for preservation.

▼ English Electric Class 40 1Co-Co1

Seen near Copy Pit at the very end of steam in 1968 is an early EE Type Class 4 diesel loco hauling a short goods train. No number is visible here, but it's still an excellent period shot.

STILL WITH DIESEL TRACTION BUT A BIT MORE COLOURFUL

▶ **The Western Pullman at Paddington station, London, in May 1963**

This class of special trains numbered five sets with six or eight carriages per set. The six-carriage sets went to the London Midland and the Western Regions, and the eight-carriage sets went to the Western Region. They were specifically first-class luxury trains, built by Metropolitan Cammell between 1960 and 1972 and better known as Blue Pullmans because of their unusual Nanking Blue paint scheme. The British Transport Commission had acquired the full equity of the private Pullman Car Company (PCC) in June 1954, and the company was nationalised and incorporated into British Rail. In 1966 the Midland Pullman was withdrawn and transferred to the Western Region as it could not compete with the newly electrified lines. All of them were withdrawn in 1972, and none were preserved. The trains were not outstanding and suffered from quite a few problems. They were, however, an example of the possibility of an inter-city fixed multiple unit train service, and as such led to the feasibility of the InterCity 125, which was successful.

◀ **Type 4 Class 45 1Co-Co1 (Peak) No. D96**

A brand new member of the Peak Class 45 1Co-Co1 Type 4 D96 at Trafford Park MPD in 1961. It was built at Crewe Works during April 1961 and given the TOPS number 45101 in March 1973. The locomotive was withdrawn in November 1986 and scrapped at Vic Berry of Leicester in October 1988.

▼ Prototype Class 47

A prototype locomotive on test on 24 September 1964 at Warrington heading north. The main prototypes for this highly successful class were *Falcon,* built by Brush, and *Lion,* by the Birmingham Carriage and Wagon works. The number here is not known.

▲ Brush Type 4 No. D1756

At Shrewsbury station in 1965 is a new British Rail/Brush Sulzer Type 4 Co-Co diesel of Class 47/48. D1756 is part of this massive class of diesel locomotives. It was built at the Brush Falcon Works and released into traffic on 4 September 1964. In February 1974 it was given the TOPS number 47162, and it was withdrawn in January 1987 and scrapped at Crewe Works four months later. To the right is a three-car set of Craven DMUs.

▲ EE Type 4 Class 40 No. D332

A carefully posed shot of English Electric Type 4 Class 40 D332 on a northbound passenger train at Preston station in 1966 with what looks like a cattle wagon behind the engine, though I doubt it can be. The locomotive was built at the EE/VF and introduced in February 1961. In 1974 it received its TOPS number 40132. It was withdrawn in March 1982 and scrapped at V. Berry, Leicester, in January 1987.

◄ Brush Type 4 Co-Co Class 50 No. D410

An overnight view of Type 4 Co-Co Class 50 D410 at Crewe station. It was a member of a class of fifty locomotives built by EE/VF between 1967 and 1968 on an initial ten-year lease from English Electric Leasing. They were specially for use on passenger trains between Crewe and Scotland before electrification was completed. On completion of the lease, they were purchased outright by BR. Once electrification was completed to Glasgow, the locomotives were transferred to the South West to allow for the withdrawal of the remaining diesel hydraulics. They were not very reliable and were nicknamed 'Hoovers' because of the noise they made. D410 was introduced in March 1968, and in March 1974 it was given the TOPS number 50010 and at the same time named *Monarch*. It was withdrawn from Laira depot in Plymouth in February 1987 as the first of the class to be withdrawn, and Coopers of Plymouth scrapped it in May 1992.

► Sulzer Type 2 Class 25/2
No. D5274

Class 25/2 No. D5274 on a hopper train at Heaton Mersey station in 1964. This was one of a class of 327 locomotives built between 1961 and 1967. This locomotive was built at Derby Works and introduced in December 1963. It was given the TOPS number 25087 in February 1974, was withdrawn in September 1980 and scrapped at Swindon Works during April 1981.

◄ EE Type 4 Co-Co Class 40 No. D213 *Andania*

A locomotive that is now preserved hauling its train through Warrington station southbound in 1962. It was built at EE/VF and introduced in June 1959. The locomotives with the numbers within D210 to D235 (except D226) were intended for use on express trains into Liverpool. As a result of this, they were named after ships in the shipping companies that were based there. D213 was named after a Cunard ship in June 1962. In March 1974 it was given the TOPS number 40013. It was withdrawn in October 1984 and purchased by the South Yorkshire Railway Society. At the time of writing, it is in beautiful condition and being used by Locomotive Services (TOC) Ltd.

▼ Class 47 Type 4 No. D1534

This locomotive was heading north towards Dallam MPD in 1964. In January 1974 it received the TOPS number 47426. It was built by Brush and introduced in August 1963. It was withdrawn in December 1992 and scrapped in May 1997 at MRJ Philips, Old Oak Common MPD.

► English Electric Type 4 Co-Co Class 50 No. 50022 *Anson*

Bristol Temple Meads on a wet day in 1978 and 50022 *Anson* stands at the platform with a train of blue and white carriages. The engine was built at EE/VF during May 1968 and introduced as D422. In March 1974 it was given the TOPS number 50022 and in March 1974 named *Anson*. It was withdrawn in August 1988 and scrapped at V. Berry, Leicester, in May 1989.

▼ English Electric Type 4 Co-Co Class 50 No. 50027 *Lion*

Also pictured at Bristol Temple Meads, the locomotive below doesn't compare well with *Anson* above: it is not in good condition and could do with a visit to the paint shop. But despite this, it had a better future! It was built at EE/VF and introduced in June 1968 with the number D427, given the TOPS number 50027 in January 1974 and the name *Lion* in May 1978. It was withdrawn in July 1991, but now the good bit: in January 1992 it was bought by a private individual and was preserved on the Mid Hants Railway. Soon after it went to the North Yorkshire Moors Railway, where it remained for seventeen years before returning to Mid Hants.

▲ **English Electric Type 4 Co-Co Class 50 No. 50045** *Achilles*

Bristol Temple Meads in 1978 and a last look at another Class 50, this time 50045 and its train of blue and white carriages. The engine was built at EE/VF and was introduced in November 1968 as D445. It received the TOPS number 50045 in March 1974 and the name *Achilles* in April 1978. It was withdrawn in December 1990 and scrapped at BR Laira.

◄ **Type 4 Co-Co Br Peak Class 45 No. 45076**

Standing at the platform at Bristol Temple Meads in 1978 is Class 45 45076. It was built at BR Crewe Works and introduced in December 1961 as D134. In January 1975 it received the TOPS number 45076, was withdrawn in November 1986 and cut up at MC Metals, Glasgow, in March 1994. On the adjoining platform is a set of Metro Cammell DMUs.

◄ **Birmingham RCW Type 2s Bo-Bo Class 33 Nos 33012 and 33008**

Still enjoying the day at Bristol Temple Meads in 1978, and here we have a double-headed passenger train. The lead engine, 33012, was built at the Birmingham Carriage and Wagon Company and introduced as D6515 in July 1960. It was withdrawn on 23 September 1987 and reinstated in January the following year. It has now been preserved and is owned by the 71A Locomotive Group based at the Swanage Railway. The name added during preservation was *Lt Jenny Lewis RN* (the first female pilot or observer to die at sea in an aircraft crash; her body was never found).

The second engine is 33008, which had the same builder and was introduced in May 1960 as D6508. In April 1974 it received the TOPS number 33008, and in April 1980 the name *Eastleigh*. It was withdrawn from Stewarts Lane in February 1967. It is now preserved and on the East Somerset Railway.

▶ **An unknown Sulzer Class 45**
A good selection of diesel power at Severn Tunnel Junction in 1978 as a Sulzer Type 4 passes down the centre with a train.

◄ English Electric Type 1 Bo-Bo Class 20s Nos 20177 and 20173

Still at Severn Tunnel Junction in 1978, and this time we have the numbers of the two Class 20s 20177 and 20173, both in a poor state and attached to a short coal train. Both were built at EE/VF, with 20177 introduced in November 1966 with the number D8177 and given the TOPS number 20177 in 1974. It was withdrawn in July 1993 and in June 2002 went into preservation at the Somerset and Dorset Railway. This was only for spares though and by 2017 it had outlived its usefulness and was conveyed to C.F. Booth, Rotherham, for scrapping. The second Class 20, 20173, was built by the same company and introduced as D8173 in November 1966. It received two TOPS numbers, firstly 20306 in April 1986 and then 20173 nine months later. It was withdrawn on 4 February 1991 and scrapped at M.C. Metals, Glasgow, a year later.

▼ Class 47 No. 47131

No. 4711 passes through Severn Tunnel station in 1978 with a train of tanks. It was built in March 1964 by Brush Traction at Loughborough and introduced with the number D1722. It was withdrawn in February 1987 and scrapped in June 1988 at V. Berry, Leicester.

◀ **Diesel mechanical shunter Class 08 No. 08756**

Shunter 08756 is attached to a guards van and a parcels van at Bristol Temple Meads station in 1978. It was built at Horwich Works for BR in 1961 and introduced as D3924. In December 1964 it was given the TOPS number 08756. It is now preserved at the Weardale Railway, Wolsingham.

▶ **Shunter Class 08 No. 08940**

A train of new tanks being shunted at Severn Tunnel Junction yards by diesel mechanical shunter 08940. The engine was built at Darlington Works, going into service in June 1962 as D4170. The TOPS number was fitted in April 1974. It was withdrawn on 31 January 2003 and scrapped at S. Norton, Liverpool, two months later.

▲ **Diesel shunter 0-6-0 No. D3533**

It is a wet night at Crewe station in 1964, but ideal for a classic photograph as diesel shunter D3533 hauls a train into the station. The locomotive was built at Derby Works and introduced in July 1958. In July 1974 it was given the TOPS number 08418, was withdrawn in March 1982 and reinstalled in June 1982. It can now be found working for the West Coast Railway Company at the Carnforth depot.

MORE UP-TO-DATE MOTIVE POWER

That day, 11 August 1968, has passed now, leaving BR to get on with conveying passengers without the help of steam traction. Even preserved steam had been banned from the main line forever. Well, that rule was relaxed in 1971, and classic trains were once again allowed on to the main line. But we had a British Railways Board and the mixed design of electric and diesel traction had, in the main, been sorted out. More problems were waiting in the wings, though: one of them is currently parked up at the Crewe Heritage

Centre in the form of the APT. The days of solo locomotives of any type of power were coming to an end for passenger work. Mainline passenger haulage continued for a while at the beginning of the 1970s, but soon only goods traffic, breakdowns and minor lines would have an independent locomotive at the head of a passenger train. So we will catch a glimpse of the independent locomotives at work before the onset of power cars that started successfully with the InterCity 125, and that will be covered in the next chapter.

▲ **Class 37 Nos 37402 and 37423**

Two members of Class 37 at York in July 2013, both in Direct Services Livery. EE/VF built 37402 and it was introduced in April 1965. The pre-TOPS number was D6974 and after that 37423. In December 1985 it was named *Oor Wullie*. It now carries the name *Stephen Middlemore 23.12.1954 to*

8.8.2013. It is still in service. EE/VT also built the second locomotive, 37423. Its pre-TOPS number was D6996 and later 37296. It was introduced in July 1965. In January 1986 it was named *Sir Murray Morrison 1874 to 1948*. It now carries the name *Spirit of the Lakes*. It is also still in service.

◀ **Intercity Class 90 electric loco No. 90007**

Manchester Piccadilly station in 1995 as Class 90 90007 in 'Swallow' livery awaits with its train at the platform. This locomotive was built at BREL Crewe and introduced in April 1988. It was later named *Sir John Betjeman* and is still in service.

▼ **Class 86 Electric loco and Class 47 diesel loco**

A typical sight at Manchester Piccadilly station in 1995 with two locomotives, both in 'Swallow' livery, awaiting departure with their respective trains.

► Virgin Class 90 electric loco No. 90014

At Manchester Piccadilly station in 1987 and in Virgin livery is A Class 90 90014. It was built at BREL Crewe and went into service in October 1984. In March 1990 it was named *The Liverpool Phil*, and is still in service.

▼ Class 390 Virgin Pendolino

A five-car unit heads south at Acton Bridge in 2015. Currently leased to Virgin from Angel Trains, the Pendolino has to be described as a success. They are electric multiple units built by Alstom and incorporating Italian Fiat Ferroviarias tilting train Pendolino technology. It is one of the fastest multiple units in Britain, with an ability to travel at 140mph but restricted to 125mph.

▲ Class 60 No. 60065

It is 2013 and a Class 60 locomotive 60065 heads south at Acton Bridge station with a goods train. Brush/Mirrlees built the locomotive at Brush Traction Loughborough and it was introduced between 1989 and 1993. It originally carried the name *Kinder Scout* but now has the name *Spirit of Jaguar* and is still in service.

◄ EWS Class 67 No. 67028 at York

No. 67028 seen with a classic train in July 2013. It was built during 1999 and 2000 for EWS by Alstom in Valencia, Spain, and is one of the few unnamed engines in the class.

British Rail decided that for many reasons the current stock needed updating. It was still losing money as road traffic became the preferred option and the customers had to be tempted back – not an easy task. Locomotives hauling carriages were outdated and countries such as Japan were leading the way with extremely fast multiple unit trains. However, countries including Japan and others had what we did not: lines that ran in a straight line. Our railway infrastructure had hardly changed since it was built, and when it was built it was in a piecemeal fashion. There were many curves and obstacles in the way, and this could not easily be changed. It was decided to invest in unique multiple unit trains that would tilt into the curves at high speed.

Work had already begun with the canting of rails on bends to allow trains to go around them more quickly and experts had been brought in to take the plan further. In 1964 a British Rail Research Division had moved into the Railway Technical Centre in Derby to improve the reliability and efficiency with the hopeful bonus that it would also reduce the costs that, despite nationalisation, were still far too high. Work on the Advanced Passenger Train (APT) had begun.

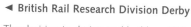
◄ **British Rail Research Division Derby**

The decision to design and build an APT was made in January 1969 and the first thing that needed to be acquired was funding for the project, which proved difficult. The already hard-up British Railways Board could not afford it: the Tokyo–Osaka train in Japan carried 120 million passengers a year and BR's busiest line, the West Coast Main Line, just 6 million, so not every participant felt that a lot could be spent on the new train. The Ministry of Transport was approached, and finally, in 1971, it was agreed that BR would pay half and the Ministry of Transport the other half. What was required was a train powered by overhead electrics that could travel at least 155mph, cornering 40 per cent faster than expresses of the period. The project commenced, and many problems arose. The plan to put the engine in the middle of the train to equalise the weight meant that there was no link between the carriages, and thus the train would need two buffet cars and more staff. Empire building detracted from the work and BR, together with other agencies, was getting a bit fed up.

The idea that the best train would be multiple units with power cars at each end was still the favourite, placing the engines out of the way underneath the carriages. This was not new; the smaller diesel and electric railcars worked the same way, as did tramcars and the Blue Pullman. Work started on this interim plan and from it was born the far more successful InterCity 125, also known as the High-Speed Train or HST.

▲ **The APT 37 0003**

Work on the APT still limped along, with long delays in construction and planning; for instance, it was discovered that two APTs passing each other from opposite directions on a bend were likely to connect as both leaned towards each other. In 1980 the APT team was disbanded, leaving onward work for other agencies, at this time the project had been running for ten years with no train yet in service. Pressure came from all sides, and eventually, the government demanded that this 'money pit be put into service', despite the ongoing problems. On 7 December 1981, the press were invited to ride on the train from Glasgow to London, during which a record of four hours fifteen minutes was set. The press was not interested; they were too busy enduring a sensation similar to seasickness as the train rolled around the bends. They were not happy, although the free food and drink probably contributed to the queasiness, and the train became a laughing stock as, among other things, it was labelled a 'queasy rider'. Finally, the APT-P trains went into service in mid 1984, bearing

in mind that the InterCity 125s had entered service in 1976 and were a great success. They were diesel and although fast at 125mph they were slow enough to travel virtually anywhere in the network.

By 1985–86 the APTs had been withdrawn, broken up or sent to museums. One of them is the star turn at the Crewe Heritage Centre, with the public able to view the train and the exhibits on weekends and bank holidays (at the time of writing). Another is at Locomotion, the National Rail Museum at Shildon.

There was still a need, however, for new high-speed locomotives and upgraded infrastructure to take them. In early 1990 work started on what was to be an InterCity 250 consisting of a Class 93 electric locomotive, nine coaches and a Driving Van Trailer (DVT). In 1992 the project was cancelled due to the coming privatisation and a shortage of funding. Later along came the Pendolino with Fiat Ferroviarias tilting ability. That, like the InterCity 125 and the later trains powered by DVTs, is a success story.

▲ **InterCity 125 Class 253 No. 253040 power car**

Seen here near Didcot in 1978 is a new member of the highly successful class of diesel multiple unit stock built at British Rail Engineering, the InterCity 125. This power car was one of thirteen built between 1978 and 1979 for the BR Western Region as a set of nine cars. Like the following example, this was one of twenty-six sets in service on the BR Western Region.

▶ **InterCity 125 Class 253 No. 253026 power car**

An InterCity diesel electric set in 1978. The class was built from 1975 to 1982 as an interim measure until the APT was ready for use. It never was, and this interim form of locomotive proved a great success, so much so that many are still in use on the privatised rail network at the time of writing in 2018. That is around forty-two years since they first appeared.

► Class 82 Mk4 Driving Van Trailer (DVT) No. 82228

Based on the InterCity 125, this large class followed them to work the high-speed passenger trains. The locomotive, driving van trailer and train remained together and the days of locomotive-hauled passenger trains were starting to be a thing of the past. Seen with its train at York station in July 2013 is 82228 in East Coast livery. It was built in 1988 by Metro Cammell for Virgin Trains and is currently in operation with Virgin Trains East Coast.

▼ Class 175/1 Coradia 1000 No. 175115

This three-car unit arrives on the Chester service at Helsby in 2017. The class was built by Alstom Birmingham between 1999 and 2001. It is still in service.

▲ **Class 350/1 No. 350103 Desiro 4 Car EMU**

Seen at Acton Bridge in 2016, this four-car DMU is on the regular Birmingham New Street to Liverpool Lime Street service. Siemens built the class for the rolling stock leasing company Angel Trains.

▶ **Bo-Bo Class 67 No. 67010**

Seen at Holyhead station on 14 July 2018 is this Alstom/General Motors locomotive. It was built between 1999 and 2000 in Valencia Spain as sub-contractors for General Motors. It is in DB Cargo UK livery, and although built as a freight engine, it is hauling a passenger train.

◄ Class 66/5 No. 66541

Again at Acton Bridge, a Class 66/5. This locomotive was built by General Motors Electro-Motive Division (EMD) in November 2001 and delivered in Freightliner green. Its depot is Leeds Midland Road TMD.

▼ Class 66/5 No. 66570

Another of these new and powerful goods engines, built by General Motors Electro-Motive Division (EMD) in December 2003.

► Class 68 No. 68025 *Superb*

A passenger train hauled by 68025 on the West Coast Main Line. It is a locomotive built by Vossloh Espana, Albuixech (Valencia), Spain, during September 2014. Allocated to Kingmoor Yard, Carlisle, here it is on a test train while virtually new, with a fellow class member at the rear. The locomotive displays the name *Superb* and is passing through Acton Bridge station while the crew train on the way to Carlisle.

▼ Mk 3 Driving Van Trailer (DVT) 82308

This large class of DVT locomotives followed the success of the InterCity 125s and three of them were obtained by Arriva Trains Wales, mainly for the Gerallt Gymro Premier Service between Holyhead and Cardiff. This is an example and carries the Arriva livery. It is seen at Holyhead station on 14 July 2018.

▲ **Class 66/7 No. 667130**

No. 66713 was built in May 2003 by General Motors EMD and given the name *Forest City*. It was seen at Darlington on 31 August 2018.

12 PRESERVED LINES AND STOCK

As previously mentioned, the actions of those whose aim it was to preserve as many steam engines and other period traction together with lines to run them on are deserving of much praise. Without them, we would now have a handful of 'Historical Relics' parked cold in museums like the bones of prehistoric animals. All BRB wanted to do was look to the future, and the future was not steam driven.

As you will see reading the histories of many of the locomotives in this chapter, they were fortunately not scrapped but stored by Dai Woodham at the Barry scrapyard, for which he received the MBE. Over the years they were removed and returned to their original condition. We have a lot to thank the many volunteers and professionals involved in the preservation societies for. So this final chapter is dedicated to them, with thanks for their hard work that we can all enjoy.

Lift your glasses and make a toast to 'the hard-working preservationists'.

◀ **Jubilee Class No. 45699 *Galatea***

Galatea was designed by Stanier and built at Crewe Works in 1936. It was withdrawn from Shrewsbury in November 1964. In January 1965 it was taken to Barry scrapyard, where it remained until April 1980, when it was purchased and preserved. After an extensive period of rebuilding it was returned to steam in April 2013. It is seen with the authors aboard launching the last book, *Remembering Steam*, which commemorated fifty years since the end of steam in photographs. The train is the 'Cumbrian Mountain Express', which is also commemorating fifty years since the end of steam, or the 'Fifteen Guinea Special'.

► BR Brush Type 4 Co-Co Class 47/48 No. 47712 *Lady Diana Spencer*

No. 47712 *Lady Diana Spencer* seen at Crewe Heritage Centre on 6 June 2018, where it is preserved. It was built at Brush Falcon works, going into service on 1 August 1966. The Type 4 was originally numbered D1948 and received its first TOPS number, 47505, in February 1974 and then number 47712 in September 1979. In April 1981 it was named *Lady Diana Spencer* in a ceremony at Glasgow Queen Street station performed by Sir Peter Parker, chairman of the British Railways Board. It is now painted in Scot Rail livery. Since retiring from BR in 2008 it has been allocated several names, including *Prince Charles Edward*, *Dick Whittington* and (planned but fortunately not fitted!) *Sir Jimmy Saville*, then *Artemis*, *Pride of Carlisle*, and then thankfully in 2016 it was returned to *Lady Diana Spencer*, the name it now bears.

► BR 2Kv Class 87 No. 87035 *Robert Burns*

No. 87035 is preserved at the Crewe Heritage Centre, where it was seen on 6 June 2018. It was built at BREL Crewe and introduced in October 1974, although it did not go into service until August 1976. All of this small class has been either exported to Bulgaria, scrapped or preserved, of which *Robert Burns* is one. It was handed over on 10 September 2005.

▲ 8F 2-8-0 No. 48151

Helsby station in Cheshire during 2013 as 8F 48151 hauls 'The Welsh Mountaineer'. The locomotive was built at Crewe Works during September 1942 and allocated to Grangemouth. Its last shed was Northwich, where it was engaged on the limestone trains from Buxton. In January 1968 it was withdrawn and sent to the Barry scrapyard in South Wales. where it remained for more than eight years. In 1975 it was purchased by the Embsay and Bolton Abbey Steam Railway in Yorkshire, eventually being purchased by David Smith, and after a heavy overhaul returned to steam on the Midland Railway at Butterley. At the time of writing, it is on mainline service with West Coast Railways. For part of its preserved life it carried the name *Gauge O' Guild*, the name of a model railway society. 8Fs were never named when in service with BR.

▼ B1 4-6-0 No. 61264 in the guise of 61034 *Chiru*

On the North Yorkshire Moors Railway at Grosmont in 2013 we find 61264 at the head of a period passenger train. The engine is carrying the name and number for 61034 *Chiru*, but that loco was scrapped at Drapers Neptune Street Goods yard in February 1965.

This Thompson-designed engine was originally unnamed 61264 of the same class. Built at the North British Locomotive Works at Glasgow in December 1947, its last shed was Colwick, from where it was withdrawn in November 1965. The locomotive was then used as a static boiler at Colwick until finally being withdrawn from there in 1966. It was then sent to the Woodhams scrapyard in Barry, where it remained for the next ten years until it was purchased and transported to the Great Central Railway at Loughborough for preservation. A twenty-one-year restoration project was undertaken, including extensive repairs to the boiler. These caused a delay that meant it was not under its own power until February 1997, when it hauled a train from Loughborough to Leicester and back. That was thirty years since its last appearance on the metals under its own steam.

In 1998 it moved to Carnforth and received a certificate for mainline service. It was well used over the coming years, appearing at many rail celebrations and open days and hauling classic trains. By 2008 it was taken to the LNWR at Crewe for a ten-year overhaul. On completion, it returned to the North Yorkshire Moors Railway, its current home.

No. 61264 is owned by the Thompson B1 Locomotive Trust and as well as carrying the name and number of *Chiru* during preservation, it has also carried 61005 *Impala*.

◀ **MT 4-6-0 No. 45428** *Bishop Eric Treacy*

Still on the North Yorkshire Moors Railway, Black Five 45428 approaches Goathland in 2013. Armstrong Whitworth built the Stanier-designed locomotive in October 1937. Its last shed was Leeds Holbeck, from where it was withdrawn on 31 October 1967. It remained at Holbeck for a year before travelling under its own power to the Birmingham Railway Museum at Tyseley in August 1968.

In May 1978 the famous railway photographer and Bishop of Wakefield, Eric Treacy, died of a heart attack on Appleby station on the Settle and Carlisle line. He was awaiting a rail tour hauled by 9F 92220 *Evening Star*. Perhaps as a tribute to this doyen of railway enthusiasm, 45428 was named *Bishop Eric Treacy*, a name that it has retained. The engine is now in the North Yorkshire Moors fleet of locomotives. It recently went for its seven-year boiler service but should be back on the rails this year. It will be restricted, however, to Grosmont to Whitby and Whitby to Battersby.

▶ **Churchward's 2-6-2T No. 4566**

Immaculate Small Prairie 2-6-2 tank 4566 and its set of carriages on the Severn Valley (SVR) railway. The train is carrying the board for 'The Royal Scot'. Were engines and coaches ever this shiny in BR days? This Churchward-designed engine was built at Swindon Works for the GWR in October 1924. In 1948 it could be found at Penzance, and its last shed was Plymouth Laira, from where it was withdrawn on 30 May 1962. Like many other locomotives in this chapter, it was taken as scrap to Barry scrapyard, where it remained for seven years before it was rescued and delivered to Bewdley for restoration, entering service in July 1975. The trials and tribulations of a preserved engine then began, including starring roles in cinema and TV.

◄ Castle Class 4-6-0 No. 5051 *Earl Bathurst/Drysllwyn Castle*

No. 5051 near Gloucester in 1974, running as *Drysllwyn Castle*. This Castle Class engine was built at Swindon Works in May 1936 and named *Drysllwyn Castle*. It carried this name for eighteen months until the name was transferred to Castle Class 7018 and 5051 became *Earl Bathurst*. Its final shed was Llanelli, from where it was withdrawn in May 1963 and sold to Woodham Brothers scrapyard at Barry five months later.

The renamed 7018 *Drysllwyn Castle* was built at Swindon in 1949 and withdrawn on 17 September 1963 from Old Oak Common. It was scrapped during June the following year at Cashmores of Great Bridge.

Five years after arriving at the Barry scrapyard in March 1969, 5051 *Earl Bathurst* was sold and taken to the Great Western Society at Didcot Railway Centre and into preservation. By 1979 it was restored to steam and reunited with the original name *Drysllwyn Castle*, the name that it bears today. At the time of writing, it is a static exhibit at Didcot awaiting a further overhaul.

► Class 35 B-B Hymek No. 7017

No. 7017 at Williton station on the West Somerset Railway in 1992 in a line of preserved stock. The diesel hydraulic locomotive was built by Beyer Peacock (Hymek) Ltd, Manchester, in 1962. It was withdrawn in March 1975, then spending time at Taunton and later Minehead.

◀ WC 4-6-2 No. 34027 *Taw Valley*

On the Severn Valley Railway at Bridgnorth in 2016 is this Bulleid-designed West Country/Battle of Britain 4-6-2 locomotive 34027 *Taw Valley*. The name of a river in Devon was an indication that it would be working in the West of England as opposed to those given Battle of Britain names for the Eastern section. It was built at Brighton Works with air-smoothed casing in April 1946, and in September 1957 the casing was removed to leave it as a rebuilt version of the class. It was originally allocated to Ramsgate and withdrawn in August 1964 from Salisbury and towed to Woodhams scrapyard at Barry. In 1985 it was purchased by Bert Hitchen and Brian Cooke, who delivered it to the Severn Valley Railway for restoration. This was completed two years later, and it commenced service both on the SVR and the mainline hauling classic express rail tours. A period of restoration followed, and in 2000 it was back on the rails hauling the Hogwarts Express to advertise the Harry Potter books. It is currently with the Severn Valley Railway.

▶ Manor Class 4-6-0 No. 7812 *Erlestoke Manor*

No. 7812 *Erlestoke Manor* on the SVR at Bewdley in 2015. This Collett-designed engine was built at Swindon Works in January 1939 and its first posting on nationalisation was Bristol Bath Road. It was withdrawn in November 1965 from Shrewsbury and delivered to Woodhams scrapyard in Barry. It was rescued from there in 1973 by the Erlestoke Manor Fund with the intention of returning it to working order. To this end, it was decided to purchase its sister, 7802 *Bradley Manor*, also from Woodhams, to use as spare parts for 7812. It turned out that 7802 was in good condition and too good to use for spares. By 1993 both locomotives had been restored to mainline standard and were used on the SVR. At the time of writing *Erlestoke Manor* is at Tyseley Locomotive Works undergoing further restoration and *Bradley Manor* has an operational boiler ticket to 2025.

► GER Class Y14 No. 564

An interesting and old engine on the North Norfolk Railway that looks simply beautiful. It was designed originally by T.W. Worsdell but is part of the class that was later built by J. Holden. It was built in March 1912 at Stratford Works.

Interestingly, in 1891 this workshop broke the record for building a steam engine. They built and fired a Y14 in nine hours forty-five minutes; it then lasted forty years. During its working life 564 also had the numbers 7564 and 65462. It was withdrawn on 30 September 1962. The Midland and Great Northern Joint Railway Society own it.

▼ Unrebuilt, West Country Class 4-6-2 No. 34092 *City of Wells*

No. 34092 in Ramsbottom station on the ELR (East Lancs Railway) during a Second World War event weekend in May 2018. Accompanying the footplate man is a rather well-dressed officer of the Wehrmacht, the Second World War German Army. The immaculately prepared Bulleid-designed engine was built at Brighton Works during September 1949 and was withdrawn during November 1964 to be sent to the Barry scrapyard, from where it was rescued in the 1970s. At the time of writing the locomotive is owned by the ELR.

◄ **Standard Class 4MT 2-6-0 No. 76084**

A Standard Class 4 arriving at Sheringham in 2016 on the North Norfolk Railway complete with the name of its first allocation on the buffer beam. Riddles-designed 76084 was built at Horwich Works during April 1957. The last shed was Wigan Springs Branch, from where it was withdrawn in December 1967 and transported to Woodhams yard at Barry. It remained there until January 1983, longer in fact than it had been in service with BR.

▼ **Standard Class 2-6-0 No. 76084**

No. 76084 leaving Sheringham. It was rescued and cosmetically restored, then in 1997 it was purchased by a small group of enthusiasts who became the 76084 Locomotive Company Limited. A full overhaul was started, and this was expedited by the purchase of sister engine 76077, also from Barry. The North Norfolk Railway (NNR, also known as The Poppy Line) became involved in the undertaking, provided cover and shared the costs. In 2016 the NNR started running trains to Cromer with 76084 as the star attraction. The locomotive is allowed on to the mainline network as well as the private lines. No. 76077 is currently with the Gloucester & Warwickshire Railway and is undergoing an extensive restoration.

▲ A4 4-6-2 No. 60007 *Sir Nigel Gresley*

This beautifully clean A4 was at Grosmont on the NYM in 2013. Probably one of the most famous steam engines, it was designed by Sir Nigel Gresley and was the 100th Gresley Pacific built at Doncaster Works, in November 1937. It was originally planned to name it *Bittern,* but as the 100th Gresley, it was named after the designer. Its first allocation was King's Cross and then on 23 April 1944, Grantham. Nationalisation saw it return to King's Cross and the last shed was Aberdeen Ferryhill, where it was withdrawn on 1 February 1966. Three months later it was sold to the A4 Preservation Society. The locomotive was then taken to Crewe Works for refurbishment, and this included acquiring the driving wheels and other parts from sister A4 60026 *Sir Miles Beevor* (which was later scrapped on 30 September 1967 at North Blyth).

No. 60007 *Sir Nigel Gresley* is the post-war holder of the world speed record for a steam engine, which it claimed when it travelled at 112mph (180km/h) on 23 May 1959.

Mallard broke the record in 1938 when it travelled at 126mph on 23 July 1938, like 60007 descending southwards from Stoke summit. It is fair to say though that *Mallard*'s run was a special attempt to beat the record. *Sir Nigel Gresley*'s was with a full train returning from an excursion. Alan Pegler was on the footplate in his capacity as a nominated member of the British Transport Commissions Eastern Area Board.

On preservation, it spent its time at Steamtown Carnforth and after the ban on mainline steam was lifted in 1971, *Sir Nigel* and *Union of South Africa* were the only mainline A4s. It moved bases a few times until arriving at the North Yorkshire Moors Railway in 1996, where it is still based. It is, however, at the time of writing, under restoration at the National Railway Museum at York after the boiler ticket expired in 2015 (the boiler has been taken to Llangollen for an overhaul).

▲ The Great Gathering, 2013

From 3 to 17 July 2013 the National Railway Museum at York held a commemoration of the day that 4468 *Mallard* broke the world steam record on 3 July 1938. All six of the preserved A4s were present at the event, which was enjoyed by more than 50,000 visitors from all over the world.

The locomotives were 1. 4464 *Bittern*, 2. 4468 *Mallard*, 3. 60007 *Sir Nigel Gresley*, 4. 60008 *Dwight D. Eisenhower*, 5. 60009 *Union of South Africa* and 60010 *Dominion of Canada*.

It wasn't only enthusiasts who came from across the world to celebrate *Mallard*'s record; two of the locomotives did as well. *Dwight D. Eisenhower* travelled from the USA and *Dominion of Canada* travelled from Canada. Not an easy task for these heavy locomotives.

Mallard's run was not a speed test and they had been stopped the previous year. The following details are taken from our book *Remembering Steam*.

During the press run in 1937, LMS Coronation Class Leader 6220 *Coronation*, driven by Driver T.J. Clarke, Fireman C. Lewis, Robert Riddles as the engineer and Inspector S. Miller, broke the previous record held by the LNER of 113mph by doing 114mph on the Madeley Bank north of Crewe.

Catastrophe nearly struck, however, as the train approached Crewe station. Those on the footplate were so elated that they did not notice at first that they were still doing 110mph. The train took the station's reverse curves, which had a speed limit of 20mph, at 57mph. Fortunately, the only damage inflicted was an uncomfortable ride for the passengers and some broken crockery. A truce was declared though between LMS and LNER because of the scare. This lasted until the following year when *Mallard* hit 126mph while 'trialling a new brake system'!

◄ A1 Pacific 4-6-2 No. 60163 *Tornado*

Not a preserved engine now but a brand new one. A1 Pacific 4-6-2 60163 *Tornado* is seen at Acton Bridge station in 2013. It was built mainly at Darlington Works, and the work started in 1994 and was completed in 2008. It is the only existing example of an LNER Peppercorn-designed A1 locomotive, as all the original production batch was scrapped! Fortunately, in 1990 the A1 Steam Locomotive Trust came into being, with the intention of building *Tornado* and other lost classes of steam locomotives. Thereby it undid a little of the damage caused by the shortsighted British Railways Board in the 1950s and '60s when it ruthlessly ordered the scrapping of steam locomotives on an industrial scale, some with fewer than ten years in service. In the case of the Peppercorn A1s, the whole batch of sixteen engines was scrapped before 1966 with an average age of just fifteen years.

Tornado's design is based on the Peppercorn LNER A1 but with improvements that were added as would have been, should the building of the class continued into the modern era. It is the first steam locomotive to travel at 100mph in the last fifty years. It first moved under its own power at Darlington Works on 29 July 2008; then after tests, it was approved for mainline passenger work. It is named after the RAF aircraft the Panavia Tornado. At the time of writing, *Tornado* is under repair but should be back on the mainline very soon.

► Royal Scot class 4-6-0 No. 46115 *Scots Guardsman*

No. 46115 *Scots Guardsman* at Helsby in Cheshire in 2014. This locomotive was designed by Fowler but rebuilt by Stanier at Crewe Works in 1947 with a taper boiler and curved smoke deflectors. It was originally built at the North British Locomotive Company, Glasgow, during October 1927 and its last shed was Carlisle Kingmoor, from where it was withdrawn on 1 January 1966. It did not, however, go to the scrapyard but remained at Carlisle to be used to demonstrate overhead power lines to enginemen. From there it went to the Keighly and Worth Valley Railway but was a bit too heavy for the lines and bridges there. After spending time at the Dinting museum, it was purchased by David Smith of the West Coast Railway Company and then in 2008 it was restored to mainline service. The locomotive is still on mainline duties and is based at Carnforth.

▼ 8F 2-8-0 No. 48773

Now a visit to the Engine House Museum at Highley on the Severn Valley Railway to see one of the true workhorses of the steam railway days, 8F Stanier-designed 2-8-0 48773. The locomotive was built at the North British Locomotive Works in Glasgow for the War Department in June 1940 with the number 70500.

After being finished, it was due to be sent to France. However, Hitler's troops got there first, so its trip was cancelled. Another duty beckoned as the Soviet Union entered the war and it was sent instead to Iran and given the Iran State Railways number 41109. It spent its time mainly double headed on the Trans-Iranian Railway delivering supplies to the Soviet troops, passing through some very steep gradients and scorching deserts. Fame – if you can call it that – arrived in 1942 when it collided with a camel and derailed itself! During 1944 it was converted to oil-burning and in 1946, with no more war to fight, it made another journey to the British Army's Middle East Forces in Egypt and was numbered WD 70307. For a while, it was loaned to the Egyptian State Railways but the war years of hard toil had taken their toll, and by 1948 the firebox needed replacement. Plans to scrap the engine were then made but luck intervened, and it was not scrapped but brought back to

the UK and repaired at Derby Works. After this, in 1954 it received another number, WD 500, and was allocated to the Longmoor Military Railway. In 1957 it was bought by British Rail and given the number 48773.

It remained in service to the end of steam and was allocated to Rose Grove in 1968. It then took part in the 'Grand Finale of Steam' on the Trans Pennine route via Copy Pit summit and then following this worked the LCGB 'Farewell to Steam Tour' on 4 August 1968. On 4 January 1969, it arrived at the Severn Valley Railway direct from BR ownership and into preservation. Since then it has clocked up more miles than any other SVR engines.

On 27 September 1986, 48773 was dedicated as a memorial to the British military railway personnel who lost their lives in the Second World War. It carries a plaque to that effect. The Stanier 8F Locomotive Society owns the loco, and after an extremely busy period in preservation it was given a cosmetic overhaul and was displayed in the Engine House Museum on the SVR, as seen. It needs a lot of work to bring it back to mainline fitness and, on 20 June 2018, it was moved to storage at Kidderminster to be in a position to commemorate an event surrounding the fifty years since the end of steam on BR. 8F 48773 is a true hero of the railways.

► Manor Class 4-6-0 No. 7802 *Bradley Manor*

Another Severn Valley Railway locomotive is 7802 *Bradley Manor*, seen here hauling a classic train in chocolate and cream GWR livery. It was built at Swindon Works for the GWR in January 1938 and withdrawn from Shrewsbury on 30 November 1965. As mentioned earlier, it was delivered to Woodhams scrapyard in Barry and bought from there for parts to be used in the overhaul of *Erlestoke Manor*. It turned out that *Bradley Manor* was in good condition – too good to use for spares.

▼ B12 4-6-0 No. 8572

B12 4-6-0 *8572* is owned by the M&GNJR (Midland and Great Northern Joint Railway Society). It is based at the North Norfolk Railway and is seen here in 2016 at Sherringham. It was built for the LNER in 1928 by Beyer Peacock Company, one of a batch of ten engines, the last of the class and the only one to be preserved.

◀ The Roundhouse at SBR

The Slatford Barn Railway at Tamworth in summer 2014 with an interesting and extensive number of narrow gauge locomotives on view. It is privately owned by Graham Lee, the former chairman of LH Group Services Ltd, a company providing services to rail freight and passenger transit. It has approximately thirty-nine steam engines, twenty-four diesel engines, eight petrol locomotives, one compressed air locomotive, three electric locomotives, eleven railcars and one tram. An impressive stable for sure.

▼ GWR 4-6-0 No. 7903 *Foremarke Hall*

This GWR Hall is seen here at Toddington in 2016 on the GWR (Gloucester and Warwickshire Railway). The Hawksworth-designed locomotive was built at Swindon Works in April 1949 and allocated to Old Oak Common. It was withdrawn from Cardiff Dock in June 1964. From there it was conveyed to Woodhams scrapyard in Barry, where it remained until purchased by a group of enthusiasts in June 1981. It was conveyed to the Swindon and Cricklade Railway in Wiltshire for rebuilding. By 2003 it was complete and made its first public appearance on 20 September at the twenty-fifth anniversary celebrations of the S & CR. *Foremarke Hall* is most likely to be the only member of the class in existence, as 7927 *Willington Hall* is being used as a donor for the building of the new Grange and County Class locos.

► **SECR P Class 0-6-0T No. 323**
Bluebell

Built at Ashford Works in 1910 and designed by Wainwright, this little engine was compared to the LBSCR Terriers. Only eight of them were built, but four of them were preserved; not many steam classes were so lucky. It was withdrawn in June 1960 and went straight to the Bluebell Railway, where it still resides.

◄ **Churchward's 2-8-0 No. 2857**

Bridgnorth on the Severn Valley Railway, and we can see one of Churchward's 2-8-0 GWR engines built at Swindon Works in May 1918. Its last shed was Neath, from where it was withdrawn on 30 April 1963. It was then stored for a while before being taken to our old favourite Woodhams scrapyard in Barry. It remained there until 1971, when members of the Seven Valley Railway set up the 28XX Fund with the intention of purchasing one of the remaining fourteen engines. Inspections revealed that 2857 was in the best condition and it was for sale at £3,500. But money was slow in coming forward, and could not compete with the gradually rising cost of the engine. Here lies an example of what hard-working heroes were involved in the purchase of locomotives for preservation. That was even before work on the actual preservation could start. By June 1974 the price was £5,250 and they managed to purchase it before the price went up to £6,500 plus £250 VAT. The engine was eventually taken to the Severn Valley Railway, and after much more hard work in raising funds, restoration started in June 1976. On 9 September 1979, the hard work was justified and the engine steamed for the first time. Running repairs were carried out during the following years, and further heavy repairs were needed by 1983. Since then 2-8-0 *2857* has become a hard-working member of the Severn Valley Railway. It is now proudly owned by the 2857 Society at the SVR.

◄ Q6 0-8-0 No. 63395

Q6 63395 heads up the grade to Goathland on the North Yorkshire Railway in 2013. This Raven-designed locomotive was built at Darlington Works during December 1918 and was allocated to Blaydon on the North Eastern Railway with the number 2238. In 1946 it received the LNER number 3395 and then the BR number 63395. It was withdrawn from Sunderland on 9 September 1967 and moved to Tyne Dock shed to await preservation. It was the last Q6 in service when withdrawn. In April 1968 it was purchased by the North Eastern Locomotive Preservation Group and then awaited restoration (it was the last Q8 to be overhauled for BR at Darlington in 1965, so the work needed was not quite so demanding). It eventually started work on the new North Yorkshire Moors Railway in June 1970.

▶ 2800 Class and 8F under BR 2-8-0 No. 2857

No. 2857 was designed by George Jackson Churchward and built at Swindon Works in 1918 for heavy goods work on the GWR. It was withdrawn from Neath on 30 April 1963 and delivered to the Barry scrapyard. It was purchased from there on 20 May 1974 and conveyed to the Severn Valley Railway. After restoration it was first steamed on 9 September 1979. It was seen on the SVR at Bridgenorth in 2016.

► **On the V of R (Vale of Rheidol) 2-6-2 tank No. 9 *Prince of Wales***

A look at narrow gauge with a visit to Devils Bridge on the Vale of Rheidol railway in 2013. This now popular tourist attraction was opened in 1902 to carry pit props in the South Wales valleys and lead ore from the Rheidol Valley, as well as timber and passengers. It runs between Aberystwyth and Devils Bridge, part of British Railways. It was the only steam-operated line to be permitted when steam on BR ended in 1968 and the first BR line to be privatised, from 1968 to 1989.

It became part of the Great Western Railway in January 1922 when its then owner, the Cambrian Railway, was absorbed. In 1923 the GWR was to rebuild the old *Prince of Wales*, but records show that it actually built a brand new engine, the one shown in the photo, in 1924, No. 9 *Prince of Wales*. The carriages were built in 1938 and are still in service today. On privatisation in 1949, the line became part of the Western Region of BR, and the engines and carriages were given new BR logos; however, in the 1980s the historical logos returned. During the 1960s all of what was the Cambrian Region was transferred to the London Midland Region, including the V of R. The railway has now been privatised and only operates between Easter and the end of October, plus February half-term and Christmas. However, this is at the time of writing and it would be best to check before visiting.

◄ **NG *G16* 2-6-2+2-6-2 No. 143**

Another Welsh narrow gauge railway, the Welsh Highland Railway, where NG *G16* 2-6-2+2-6-2 No. 143 is taking on water at Caernarvon in 2011. Beyer Peacock built the locomotive in Manchester during 1958 for the South African Railways, where it went to work at the Alfred County Railway. The company overhauled the locomotive before it was shipped back to Britain to be put to work on the Welsh Highland Railway based at Caernarvon in September 1998. In 2009 it started a ten-year overhaul, at which time it was converted back to coal firing. In July 2011 it returned to service in the new green livery.

◄ GWR 2-6-2 T Large Prairie tank No. 5164

This light engine at Bewdley on the Severn Valley Railway is an immaculate Collett-designed 2-6-2T. It was built at Swindon Works for the GWR in November 1930 and withdrawn on 30 March 1963 from Pontypool Road. Sent to the Barry scrapyard, it was rescued by the SVR on payment of £2,250. It still resides, there having been beautifully restored.

▼ GWR 4200 Class 2-8-0 Tank No. 4277 *Hercules*

The snow falls gently on to the hot boiler of Churchward-designed GWR 2-8-0 Tank engine 4277 as it heads into the Kingsley and Frogall station on the CVR (Churnet Valley Railway). The date is 3 February 2018. Built at Swindon Works and going into service in April 1920, it was withdrawn from Aberbeeg on 30 March 1964 to be sent to Barry scrapyard. It was rescued from there in June 1986 and is now owned by the Dartmouth Steam Railway. It was on loan to the CVR until 2018, when it was returned as the boiler ticket had run out. It did not carry a name when in service, but in preservation it has been called *Hercules*.

► 9F 2-10-0 No 92214 *Cock O' the North*

No. 92214 bearing the preserved name *Cock O' the North* awaits the 'right away' at Grosmont on the North Yorkshire Moors Railway. The Riddles-designed engine was built at Swindon Works and entered service on 31 October 1959 at Canton Cardiff. It was withdrawn in September 1965 from Severn Tunnel Junction with less than six years' service. It was taken to the Barry scrapyard, where in 1980 it was the youngest engine to be sold from there. It is now owned by the Great Central Railway and has a boiler certificate lasting another five years.

▼ A3 4-6-2 No. 60103 *Flying Scotsman*

Seen here on the 'Blackpool Belle' on 8 September 1966 at an unknown location is the iconic *Flying Scotsman*. A locomotive that has been well recorded, it once belonged to Alan Pegler with a permit to use the main lines until 1971 – the only engine to have such a privilege. It then went on US and Australian tours.

► **Hall Class 4-6-0 No. 4930 *Hagley Hall***

Simmering just off the main line at Bridgnorth on the Severn Valley Railway in 1968 is the immaculate Collett-designed Hall Class 4-6-0 *Hagley Hall*. It was built at Swindon Works and went into service in May 1929, being withdrawn in December 1963 for delivery to the Barry scrapyard. It was rescued ten years later by the Severn Valley Railway, withdrawn in 1986, then spent eight years as a static exhibit at the McCarthur Glen retail park in Swansea. It is currently being restored and is expected back in service in 2020.

▲ **MN 4-6-2 No. 35028 *Clan Line***

An unknown location but a view of Modified Merchant Navy Class 35028 *Clan Line* hauling 'The Red Rose' on 28 April 1979. One of the most famous of the preserved engines, the Bulleid-designed locomotive was built at Eastleigh Works, going into service in December 1948. Withdrawn from service in July 1967, the following month it became the property of the Merchant Navy Locomotive Preservation Society (MNLPS) for the sum of £2,200 (roughly £50,000 today). With many miles now on the clock, it has just received another overhaul, this time at Crewe, and *Clan Line* is once again on main line duties.

▲ **Hall Class 4-6-0 No. 6960** *Raveningham Hall*

Framed neatly under a bridge, Modified Hall Class *6960 Raveningham Hall* departs Arley for Kidderminster on the Severn Valley Railway in 1968. Developed by Hawksworth on the Collett design, it was built at Swindon Works and went into service on 6 March 1944. Withdrawn in June 1964, it was sent to the Barry scrapyard and rescued by David Edleston of Derby in 1972. He sold it to Steamtown Carnforth, and it was based at the SVR before being sold to businessman Jeremy Hosking in 1996. It can now be found at the West Somerset Railway.

◄ BR Drewry-designed 0-6-0 diesel shunter D2090

D2090 was built at Doncaster Works in 1960 and withdrawn on 18 July 1976. It is now in the National Collection at Locomotive, Shildon.

▼ No 29, 0-6-2T

Already featured in monochrome, this locomotive was designed by Kitson and Company and built by Hunslet for the Lambton Railway. It was delivered in 1904 and was operated on the Lambton Hetton & Joicey Colliery lines. It was withdrawn in 1969, then purchased by the NYMR and returned to steam in 2013. However, it was taken out of service in 2014 due to a cracked cylinder block. It now awaits repair and was photographed on 13 July 2014 at Pickering station.

► **Ivatt Class 4MT 2-6-0 No. 43106**

Simmering quietly at Bewdley on the SVR in 2015 is a 'Flying Pig', well, that is an enthusiast's pet name for an Ivatt Class 4. The engine was built at Darlington Works in April 1951; it was withdrawn from Lostock Hall on 22 June 1968 and went light engine to the SVR on the day before the official end of revenue earning steam on BR, 2 August 1968. It was one of the first engines on the books. The Ivatt Class 4 Group own her.

► **Locomotive 2-4-0T No. 13 *Kissack***

The narrow gauge Isle of Man railway has been in existence since 1870. Originally it comprised the Manx Northern Railway and the Foxdale Railway, but these two companies combined in 1905 to form the Isle of Man Railway. It has since had various name changes and is now smaller but successful. *Kissack* was built in 1910 by Beyer Peacock of Manchester, as were most of the company's steam engines. It is named after one of the company directors and local politician Edward Thomas Kissack. This particular locomotive has seldom been out of service. It was seen at Douglas on 20 July 2018.

▲ **GWR 0-6-0PT Class 5700 No. 5775**

No. 5775 on the KWVR Railway, a quite famous locomotive pannier tank designed by Collett and built at Swindon Works in 1929 for the GWR. It was withdrawn from BR on 31 July 1963 and sold to London Transport. In 1969 it was sold by LT to the KWVR. Now the famous bit: this was the locomotive that starred in *The Railway Children*.

◄ **Standard Class 4 Tank 2-6-4T No. 80072**

No. 80072 was designed by Riddles and built at Brighton Works, going into service on 3 November 1953 at Plaistow. It was withdrawn on 24 July 1965 from Shrewsbury and taken to the Barry scrapyard. It remained there until 1988, and after a spell at Swindon it was moved to Llangollen for a full restoration, which took eighteen years to complete. It is owned by the 80072 Steam Loco Company and was seen at Llangollen in 2017.

► **Class 86 E3137, later *Peter Pan***

E3137 at Crewe station on 11 August 2018 on the fifty years from the end of steam on BR special train. The locomotive was built at Doncaster Works in 1965 and in January 1974 it received the TOPS Number 86259. In 1979 it was named *Peter Pan* at a ceremony at Euston station. In October 1995 when based at Longsight, Manchester, the *Peter Pan* nameplates were replaced with *Greater Manchester – The Life and Soul of Britain*. In 1999, four years after privatisation, the engine could be found in Virgin livery. In 2002 it was named *Les Ross* after the West Midlands broadcaster and rail enthusiast. The locomotive was withdrawn the following year and in 2006 Les Ross purchased the engine that bore his name. It went for an overhaul and in 2008 it hauled its first train in preservation. It is now beautifully painted in the original 1960s blue livery and bears the name *Les Ross* on one side and *Peter Pan* on the other, with the numbers to match the names.

EPILOGUE

That was a journey through our British Railways from the earliest to the latest, from the days of open trucks to our 150mph (capable) diesel and electric multiple units, from privately owned companies to nationalisation with British Railways and back again. Where do we go from here? We have tried to advance with the folly of the Advanced Passenger Train to the highly successful InterCity 125s and onwards, replacing locomotive-hauled carriages with high-speed multiple units including the ubiquitous Pendolinos, with even more modern traction in the pipeline.

Currently work is in progress on a new HS2, or High-Speed Train, although public support seems lacking and the possibility of another cancelled money pit must surely be a possibility.

The question today is, will we return to nationalisation? Well, some of the private rail companies have not exactly showered themselves in glory. At the time of writing, in certain areas the new rail timetables have led to the virtual meltdown of the system, with many cancelled trains. The travelling public is not amused in those areas, and the call for renationalisation grows.

But this book is aimed at enthusiasts in all forms of railway transport and infrastructure. Fortunately, with the hard work of the preservationists, we now have a very big private preserved railway network. I was going to list them here, but there are far too many. Suffice to say, had it been left to the British Transport Commission and the British Railways Board we would now just have a few locomotives in museums. Short-sightedness abounded at the time; in 1955, a gentleman by the name of Brigadier T.I. Lloyd thought that it would be a good idea to turn the railways into roads. Then in 1957, he published a booklet entitled *Twilight of the Railways – What Roads They'll Make*. Shortly after, he formed 'The Railway Conversion League'. The League aimed to turn the whole of the railway network in Great Britain into preserved roads! In fact, a completely new road network to run just like the, err … railways with its own maintenance, police, etc. Traffic would be strictly regulated into lanes with no overtaking. Sounds exciting, doesn't it?

I think that steam is still the biggest draw, and has been from its first venture out on wheels. Fortunately Great Britain has the biggest preserved rail network in the world, and its popularity would have stunned the naysayers of the 1950s and '60s. So get out and enjoy it; Santa and other treats for the children, candlelight suppers for the lovers and total enjoyment for everyone.